# Secrets of
# New York City

# Secrets of New York City

## Marjorie Palmer
## Photographs by Erika Larsen

# Secrets of New York City

For information address:
Silver Lining Books
122 Fifth Avenue
New York, NY 10011

Silver Lining Books and colophon are registered trademarks.

Editorial Director:    Barbara J. Morgan
Editorial Assistant:   Emily Seese
           Design:   Richard J. Berenson
                     Berenson Design & Books, Ltd., New York, NY
       Production:   Della R. Mancuso
                     Mancuso Associates, Inc., North Salem, NY

Library of Congress Cataloging-in-Publication Data is available on request.

ISBN 0-7607-3195-0

Printed and bound in the United States of America

First Edition

# CONTENTS

**Special thanks are owed to the following people
who helped make this book possible:**

Peter Basich of the NYC Department of Bridges and Tunnels
Mel and Scott Cohen, B&J Fabrics
Ellie and Richard Denker
Elise Fink of the NYC Department of Buildings
Steve Hollander
Dr. Mitchell Kahn
Jill Keefe
Juwana Montgomery, DOT Maspeth Central Shop
Steve Resnick
Bill Rancitelli
Joseph Salvo, NYC Planning Commission
Steve Schwartz
Jane Scovell
Dean Stadel
Elizabeth White and Arnold Lieber

**NEW YORK** is one of the most written about and photographed cities in the world. It's a place everyone knows about, or thinks they do. In that New York, there are palaces of finance and mansions of fashion. There are quaint pushcarts, where New Yorkers graze their way across an infinite palate of tastes. And luxury restaurants filled with beautiful people.

But there's another New York. And it's full of secrets.

Secrets, not mysteries. The stories, places, and people in this book are not shrouded and hidden. They are in plain sight. You just have to know where to look.

The secrets of the city are those wonderful things about New York that are unexpected, or that stir curiosity, or await discovery. They are the dramas that happen behind the scenes on Broadway or Wall Street. The odd things that can be found lying just around the corner on some small street, or bobbing along a city waterway, or high in the metropolitan sky.

You may be a native-born New Yorker, but you may not know that honeybees are buzzing merrily on some Manhattan rooftops and that the honey they produce is exceptionally sweet, flavored by the flowers of New York. Yes, the flowers of New York.

Perhaps you love New York theater and go often. But have you ever been to a Gypsy Robe ceremony? Have you ever even heard of it?

Or perhaps you're from out of town and always planned to see the city's sights. If you are, remember there's more to New York than what's in the guidebooks.

There are secrets.

Hollywood is Tinseltown, all make-believe, on film, larger-than-life, and distant. In New York, they do it live and life-size.

# No Business Like Show Business

**L**IKE A LOT OF THINGS IN NEW YORK, show business is right now—and in-your-face. Hollywood is Tinseltown, all make-believe, on film, larger-than-life, and distant. In New York, they do it live and life-size. The actors are there in person. So are the singers onstage at the Metropolitan Opera House, Luciano Pavarotti in Central Park, *Saturday Night Live* on television.

But achieving that immediacy takes a lot of time, energy, and people. A host of things you don't see go into making that show you're watching a transporting experience.

And of course, show business is a nation unto itself. Its various tribes maintain their own, often strange tribal rituals and traditions.

## Prop Guys: The Men Who Throw the Eggs at Alec Baldwin

**They're also the guys who aim the cakes** that land in Jimmy Fallon's face. And supply the horse's head for the Mafia bit. And the big, green ugly cabbage for Margaret Jo's fictional National Public Radio show, "Delicious Dish."

They are the guys from Hand Props, the ones whose kingdom is the *Saturday Night Live* properties cage, just sprinting distance away from the stage area of famed Studio 8-H. Their names are Steve Demmler, Tim Flynn, and Doug Neill. And no prop is too strange or too hard to find for them, no slapstick too absurd to arrange.

Does the evening's madcap mayhem require a porcupine trap? No problem. A pratfall on a can of Cheez Whiz—watch out for flying cheese bubbles! And once found or conceived, it's also their job to make sure that all else goes smoothly, propwise, during the everything-changes-at-the-last-minute, cardio-fitness workout that is a live performance of television's classic comedy showcase.

They get started on Wednesday—each and every Wednesday. Up to then, only the *SNL* writers have seen the script, but on Wednesday, there's a read-through for the various production department heads: costumes, sets, lighting, props, etc., laying out what each department

will need to do to bring the script to life. For the Hand Props guys, it means it's time to start finding or creating the items the cast members will throw, chew, step on, mangle, or otherwise use. The only problem is that the sketches are constantly being changed, says Tim Flynn. So the list of props and their onstage geography also constantly change.

Flynn tries to stay one sketch ahead of the process. He creates crude drawings of the stage layout, listing which hand props have to be where to coincide with both the script and the camera shot. Meanwhile, Doug Neill lists the props that will "decorate" each room in a sketch. Sometimes a single show will feature two or even three routines set in living rooms. Neill makes sure that the *objets* that grace a Park Avenue penthouse stay separate and apart from the doodads in a suburban tract house or the junk in a trailer park double-wide.

Overseeing it all is veteran Steve Demmler, who's been with the show since it started.

By Friday, all the props have to be in-house. Friday is the day of camera blocking, deciding every shot in the show: where the cameras will be, when, and which shots each will be responsible for.

On Saturday, the workday begins at about noon with another run-through for every sketch, this time with no stops. At eight o'clock, there's a full dress rehearsal in real time before a live audience. At this point, some sketches are typically cut from the show, and that caps it,

**For the Hand Props guys, it's time to start finding or creating the items the cast members will throw, chew, step on, mangle, or otherwise use.**

PARTS  LIFE SIZE DOLLS  STUFFE

except for some potential further writing changes. The kaleidoscopic changeability of the *SNL* script is legendary, with the writers constantly fiddling with the scripts to squeeze out the last possible laugh.

One host, Sir Ian McKellen, once mused on the irony of a classical actor like himself, "used to doing . . . plays that have been around for centuries. And here I am performing work that's only been around since yesterday afternoon. In fact," McKellen went on, "they're still writing some of the scripts right now." It can make for a nerve-racking evening.

And that's before anybody ever says, "Live from New York, it's Saturday night!"

Once those words are spoken, the prop guys are on the go every minute. It's not unusual for a single sketch to require 15 prop cues. In the confined space that is the stage of Studio 8-H, they are tightly positioned with their racks, supplying and retrieving the right prop at the right moment, making sure the stethoscope and spectacles are downstage left when the actor gets there, and that the eye patch and

**The kaleidoscopic changeability of the *SNL* script is legendary, with the writers constantly fiddling with the scripts to squeeze out the last possible laugh.**

**"Live from New York, it's Saturday night!"**
**Once those words are spoken, the prop guys are on the go every**
**minute. It's not unusual for a single sketch to require 15 prop cues.**

diamond earring are upstage right when he gets there, and that no one
in the huge television audience has any idea how it all happens.

Where do the props live? In the properties department cage just
down the hall and in an extra storage room five floors away. Enter and
see what it's like to be a professional pack rat. There are floor-to-ceiling
shelves filled with whiskey bottles, conga drums, framed diplomas from
every institution of learning on earth—most of them nonexistent—a
giant dog bone, a pair of legs, 40 flip-top jars of mustard. Forty? What
can you do with 40 flip-top jars of mustard? Hey! It's *Saturday Night Live*.

As for those flying eggs and cakes, they are meant to actually land,
splatter, and slither on the performers. There is no sleight of hand. On
very rare occasions, a mishap occurs. Flynn remembers the night he
tossed those eggs at Alec Baldwin. The eggs, for some reason, did not
break; instead, they simply bounced off the actor's torso, leaving
Baldwin without the expected comedic moment. Baldwin shot Flynn a
look, but the response he showed to the audience was as gracious as
the man is handsome.

Only in showbiz could a man regret *not* being splattered by a
raw egg.

# The Gypsy Robe:
# Does It Really Bring Good Luck?
# The Gypsies Think So

**They don't get their names in lights.** They don't get Tony awards.
In fact, they don't even get individual credit lines in the *Playbill*.
Yet they're the absolutely essential element of just about every
Broadway musical.

They're the gypsies, the dancing singers and singing dancers
who make up the chorus of a musical show and who, apart from the
musical *A Chorus Line,* which celebrated their lives, are virtually
nameless—unsung and unrecognized.

But they do have one thing that is uniquely theirs, the focus of a
Broadway ritual for decades. It's the gypsy robe, a caftanlike garment
that is a patchwork of mementos of the musical shows it has touched.
Like a Broadway gypsy, it moves from one show to the next to the next.
It ensures, or so the gypsies say, that the show will be a hit.

Does it work? Not always, but often enough to keep the tradition going.

The robe belongs to no single gypsy, and thus to all of them in some powerful way. It is deeply entrenched in Broadway lore, even though it all started as a gag. It was October 12, 1950, opening night of the musical *Call Me Madam,* starring the redoubtable Ethel Merman. A jittery chorus member in the show, one Arthur Partington, received a gift from a fellow chorus member who was appearing in the long-running hit, *Gentlemen Prefer Blondes.* The gift was "a tacky dressing gown," as even the giver, Bill Bradley, described it. But he said it brought good luck.

It worked. *Call Me Madam* was a smash hit, so Partington attached a rose from Merman's gown to the robe and sent it to a colleague in the chorus of the next new musical, *Guys and Dolls,* on its opening night. Another hit. A tradition was born.

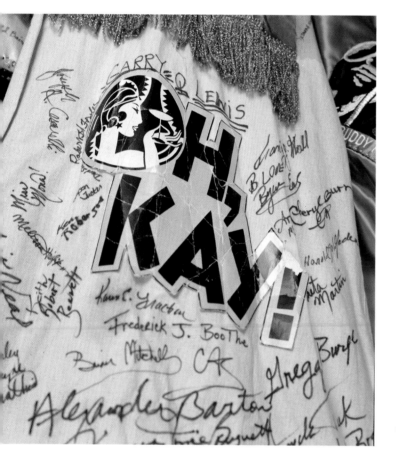

But it was haphazard, and no one was quite certain what became of robes as they filled up with mementos and disappeared. So in 1980, Actors' Equity made Terry Marone, an Equity official and former gypsy, the official keeper of the robe. It was typecasting. Marone comes as close as anyone to having been born in a trunk in the backstage of a theater.

The daughter of ballroom dancers, Marone is a veteran of ten Broadway productions and scores of road companies. She's a true gypsy who capped her performing career by serving as Equity's contract compliance monitor in the field for all things related to the chorus. Keeping the robe alive was important to her. "It is," she says, "the only thing the chorus has."

Marone soon heard about a theater buff and writer named Gloria Rosenthal, who had been chronicling the robe's journeys since 1982. In fact, she and the robe's originator, Bill Bradley, had

**The robe belongs to no single gypsy, and thus to all of them in some powerful way. It is deeply entrenched in Broadway lore, even though it all started as a gag.**

formalized the Rules of the Robe. It may be given only to a true gypsy—i.e., one with a chorus contract; it should go to the chorus member in the new show who has the most Broadway experience; and the recipient is responsible for adding the show's memento and getting cast members to sign the robe.

**It may be given only to a true gypsy; it should go to the chorus member in the new show who has the most Broadway experience; and the recipient is responsible for adding the show's memento and getting cast members to sign the robe.**

The rules also detail the ceremony for the presentation of the robe, which takes place onstage an hour or so before the opening-night curtain goes up. At that time, of course, no audience is present, just rows and rows of empty seats. Backstage, however, people are running around getting everything and everyone ready. The air is charged with pre-opening excitement.

An announcement over the P.A. system cuts through the tension. "Everybody onstage for the gypsy robe ceremony, please."

The cast gathers—not just the gypsies, but all the cast, stars, featured players, as well as the director and producer and choreographer, if they're on hand. All form a circle onstage. In the middle of the circle, wearing the robe, is the recipient from the last Broadway opening. Terry Marone introduces the robe-wearer and turns over the proceedings to him.

Flashbulbs pop as he reads out a brief history of the gypsy robe and recites its rules. Tension mounts. The circle of cast members draws together more tightly, inching closer to the robe. "The chorus member in this show who will receive the robe," the current robe-wearer intones, "is . . ." It might as well be the Tonys, with an envelope about to be opened, as a name is called.

Shrieks! Hugs! Whistling! Applause! Smiling as excitedly as any newly anointed god, the chorus member dons the robe, faces the cameras, then lopes counterclockwise around the circle of colleagues

**Shrieks! Hugs! Whistling! Applause! Smiling as excitedly as any newly anointed god, the chorus member dons the robe, faces the cameras, then lopes counterclockwise around the circle of colleagues three times, as cast members reach out to touch the robe.**

three times, as cast members reach out to touch the robe.

There are more photos: the former robe-wearer and the current robe-wearer, the current robe-wearer with various cast members. Gypsies check out the mementos for the hits and the misses: a bright yellow gloved hand from *Contact,* the stovepipe hat from *Seussical.* For every memento, there's a memory, not all of them good. "I was in that one." "Remember this one?" "Ugh. That one."

And then Terry Marone is saying that it's time to wrap it up, they've got a show to put on tonight.

The cast disperses. But the new robe-wearer still has work to do. Before the curtain rises, he will visit every dressing room, as if bringing not just luck but the blessing of a long and honored tradition, an unbroken line of Broadway gypsies.

Where do the gypsy robes go when every inch is filled? They retire to museum collections. Look for gypsy robes in the Museum of the Performing Arts in New York's Lincoln Center, at the Smithsonian on the Mall in Washington, D.C., or in the Museum of the City of New York.

## An Artist Who Paints Broadway's Costumes

**Remember the slinky zebra-striped dressing gown** Norma Desmond, once great star of silent films, wore as she slowly descended the grand staircase in *Sunset Boulevard?* Or Scar's patterned leather chaps in *Lion King?* And the so-real feline fur of Jennyanydots and Skimbleshanks in *Cats?*

As with so many theater costumes, the patterns on these legendary, one-of-a-kind outfits were not woven or printed or applied. They were painted, by a handful of specialists known as professional costume painters.

Why take the time to laboriously hand-paint a costume when so many printed patterns are already available? It's part of creating the magic, the illusion of the theater. There is no limit to what a designer can imagine or the painter create. They can call forth any image, evoke any mood, make the pattern fall just so. The only limit is their own skills.

And, in more practical terms, they can work their magic without adding weight to the garment or making it difficult to move in.

The costumes mentioned above, for example, were all painted by

**Why take the time to laboriously hand-paint a costume when so many printed patterns are already available? It's part of creating the magic, the illusion of the theater.**

Mary M., who has been creating theater costumes since 1976. It's not a profession she was trained for. Until recently, when people like Mary began teaching it, costume painting was not something you could learn in school. It is still not part of the formal art training curriculum.

Mary, a graduate of the School of Visual Arts, was teaching at a Montessori nursery school when an old friend mentioned that Brooks Van Horn, a legendary theatrical costume shop, now defunct, was looking for painters. "Why not give it a try?" the friend said.

So she took a job painting costumes for the theater, an unknown world. She mastered the job by doing it, experimenting and improvising as she learned to deal with different fabrics and with the thickened acid dyes that are the medium for painting costumes. It was also a matter of thinking in theatrical terms because, Mary soon realized, she hadn't just taken a job, she had entered an entirely new universe, the theater. And she found it "totally engrossing and totally exhilarating."

How do you paint a costume? It starts with the designer's sketch, some more detailed than others. Then the draper—the individual responsible for making the costume—the designer, and the painter together choose a fabric, and the painter creates a small sample of her work. The sample shows the painter's interpretation of the sketch, and creating it is, in Mary's view, the most interesting part of the job. It's also time-consuming—mixing the colors, testing them on the chosen fabric, working with the designer and draper to get it right.

Once the designer gives the go-ahead, the draper lays out the costume in rectangles, just like any garment pattern. Mary stretches the costume out tight on the long tables in her studio, tacks it down with pushpins, and begins to paint. She applies the paint, actually a transparent dye, using paintbrushes and sponges, among other implements, many of her own invention, to get just the effect she's after.

**"Costume painting became the thing that everybody wanted to use." The reason? "You can do anything with it," she says. "There is no limit to what the designer can imagine; the only limit is the skill of the painter."**

Costume painting is probably as old as theater itself, long used to create effects of "distress"—to make a garment look old, or worn, or dirty. But in the early years of the 20th century, and particularly under the influence of the great dancer and choreographer Nijinsky, costume painting came into its own. It was a time of "great creative ferment," in Mary's phrase, when dancers and painters and composers gloried in knocking down classical traditions by the fistful. Painters fired with the freedom to paint in new ways covered walls, furniture, theater sets, and clothing with their compositions. How could costume painting not became another pathway to expression. Not just a way to enrich the overall production but a way to make the costume itself "speak"?

In 1987, the Joffrey Ballet revived *Le Sacre du Printemps (The Rite of Spring),* a work originally created by Nijinsky for the Ballets Russes in 1913 to the music of Igor Stravinsky. Mary was in charge of coordinating the costume painting, a task that involved some half a dozen painters working full-time and flat out for two to three months to paint about 30 costumes. Researchers had spent years scouring the world for photos of the original costumes. There was a premium on getting it right, on honoring the originals and creating something fabulous for the theater. For Mary, it was a high point of her professional life.

> **"Broadway budgets no longer accommodate specialties like costume painting,"** she laments. **"It's increasingly seen as a luxury, and fewer designers use it."**

And while the process of costume painting has not changed since then, something else has. "Broadway budgets no longer accommodate specialties like costume painting," she laments. "It's increasingly seen as a luxury, and fewer designers use it." Besides, as Mary is not the first to point out, producers once concerned about quality now look only to the bottom line. "Theater producers used to be theater people," she says. "Now, increasingly, they're money people."

These days, costume painting tends to be commissioned for the more spectacular events, like the circus, Disney parades, and cruise ship entertainments. The style is "bolder," says Mary, "less subtle. It's work that has to 'read' from a distance." It is still fun, often exciting, but it can't blot out the nostalgia for an earlier era when the art of costume painting brought its own subtle magic to the theater.

## ■ She Prompts Opera Stars

**Opera singers are on the road** more than rock stars. They master scores of scores—words and music. They perform in many different productions of the same opera, learning different interpretations under different directors. Ever wonder how they remember just which line of recitative they're supposed to be singing at any one moment?

Well, they don't always remember.

Let's say it's twenty minutes into a performance of Puccini's *Tosca* at the Metropolitan Opera House. The orchestra is making music exuberantly. The diva playing the title role is singing her heart out, moving toward the tenor. Beyond the footlights, four thousand people are watching.

And the tenor, who has sung the male lead a million times, suddenly draws a complete blank. He has no clue what he's supposed to sing or do next. He's completely at a loss.

Well, not completely. Out of the corner of his eye, he glances down at a funny three-sided box that juts up from the edge of the stage. Inside it, invisible to the audience but shining like a beacon of hope, sits Jane Klaviter, one of four full-time Met Opera prompters. *"Ah! M'avvinci ne' tuoi lacci,"* Klaviter enunciates clearly and on pitch just before the tenor is supposed to sing the line. It is safe to say that the tenor's "Ah!" is as much a sigh of relief as a cry of passion.

> Ever wonder how opera singers remember just which line of recitative they're supposed to be singing at any one moment? Well, they don't always remember.

Opera singers deserve all the help they get, says Klaviter. "There is so much going on onstage." Dressed in costumes that are often heavy or constricting, opera singers must move, emote, sometimes dance or fence or fall, all the while executing the most demanding of the vocal arts. They've earned the help they get, and at the Met, as at most of the world's major opera houses, that help has traditionally been provided by the prompter.

Jane Klaviter became a prompter "by a fluke," as she puts it. A highly trained musician specializing in the operatic repertory, Klaviter was working at the renowned Dallas Opera as an assistant conductor. One night, in a drama worthy of grand opera, the prompter who served the legendary Maria Callas didn't show up, and Klaviter was called on to stand in for him. The opera, in German, was Wagner's *Flying Dutchman*. A new prompter was born.

Today, Klaviter prompts performances not only in German but in Italian, French, and Russian as well. But knowing languages and music and opera scores is only the beginning of what's required to do this job. Klaviter not only feeds singers the first few words of their next piece just before they come in, she frequently supplies the pitch as well. And since "orchestras are notorious for being behind the beat," Klaviter often snaps her fingers or claps to mark the beat.

Mostly, she talks in a normal voice, but sometimes it's necessary to shout. Not infrequently, when a singer is really befuddled, she must yell, "Look at me!" in whatever language the singer will best understand. She also uses sign language. Holding her hand up means "Stop singing!"—usually because a nervous singer has come in a bar or so too early. A finger pointing up means "You're flat; sing higher." A finger pointing down means the opposite: The singer is sharp and should lower the pitch.

Some singers may disregard the prompter entirely, although they're probably glad to know she's there, just in case. Other singers rely on the prompter constantly, turning toward the front of the stage even when the logic of the moment would have them staring passionately into their lover's eyes. It depends on the production, the conductor, and the singer's confidence. "Singers who know how to use us tend to use us wisely," says Klaviter.

**Not infrequently, when a singer is really befuddled, she must yell, "Look at me!" in whatever language the singer will best understand.**

**Klaviter remembers one singer who was "completely off—words, notes, pitch, beat: I mean everything—through an entire aria." Klaviter shouted the words and screamed out instructions, but nothing worked.**

Although the prompter's box juts up from the stage, Klaviter enters it via a subterranean set of three steps and sits on a chair that rises hydraulically. The box is narrow and cramped—it encases her like a helmet—but affords her a view of the entire stage, although her eyes are at the level of most performers' shins. Since the conductor and orchestra are behind her, two monitors show Klaviter the conductor, and two speakers let her hear the orchestra. There's a fan in the box to keep her cool, and there's a phone in case of a real emergency.

Emergencies are unlikely, but the threat of an onstage disaster is never far off. Klaviter remembers one singer who was "completely off—words, notes, pitch, beat: I mean everything—through an entire aria." Klaviter shouted the words and screamed out instructions, but nothing worked. Though such incidences are rare, the potential for their occurrence adds a level of stress to work that is already challenging, especially when a prompter must deliver as many as four performances a week.

The prompter's stress, however, is the singer's solace—for opera buffs, a fair exchange.

## "This Way, Please." The Job of a Broadway Usher

**It's a dream job,** once handed down from mother to daughter, now earned strictly on merit. It brings you into the heart of New York's theater world, but it's steady work—and there are no auditions. You get to see the best that Broadway has to offer, and for free. Better, they pay you for it.

It's being an usher at a Broadway theater, a job coveted by many but held by a lucky few.

One of the few is Rosa Balsamo, chief usher at the Virginia Theatre, a venerable theater in Manhattan. Balsamo has been an usher for decades, since the day she was a young mother looking for a job that would allow her to be at home during the day.

PLAYBILL
VIRGINIA THEATRE
THE CRUCIBLE

Now a grandmother, she is still leading people to their seats on theater nights.

Balsamo isn't the first woman to find the usher's job a godsend for a mother with children. For years, Local 306 of the International Alliance of Theatrical Stage Employees, the ushers' union, was a virtual monopoly for women who lived on the West Side of Manhattan. The theaters were within walking distance of home, ushering did not require an eight-hour day, and coming to the theater gave the women a social life. No wonder the jobs were handed down like a prized legacy.

For people who love the theater, it's a way to not just be around show business but to be a part of it. Many ushers spend their days at auditions or interviews, hoping to move from the "front of the house" to center stage. There's always that chance, after all. Barbra Streisand was a substitute usher before she got her big break.

As for people for whom the ushering job starts out as a job, love of theater seems to follow quite quickly. "We see the best performers in the world," says Balsamo. "We see theater at its best."

Not that the job is easy. Ushers work eight shows a week, with only Mondays off. There's an usher for each aisle, and they're responsible for seating hundreds of people in half an hour, taking care that nobody brings food or drinks to the seat, making sure everybody is in the right seat—comfortably and on time. They do so not just once but at every intermission as well.

**For people who love the theater, it's a way to not just be around show business but to be a part of it. Many ushers spend their days at auditions or interviews, hoping to move from the "front of the house" to center stage.**

Some ushers—two per floor—stay inside when the doors are closed to make sure no one uses a camera or video, and to be on the spot in case someone becomes ill. As chief usher, Rose Balsamo remains in the lobby during the show, seeing to it that nobody comes in off the street and attending to anybody who leaves suddenly. She's there to direct theatergoers to the rest room when nature calls or to the bar if they don't like the show. And when the curtain goes down, she's there until the house is empty, making sure everybody gets out okay.

The best show she ever ushered? She can't decide between *On Your Toes* and *Bubbling Brown Sugar*. "I love musicals," Balsamo says. "They make us happy."

# The Taste of New York

**N**EW YORK IS KNOWN AS the most ethnically diverse eating
town on earth, as well as a town that will try anything. And then,
of course, criticize it to a fare-thee-well. Both the willingness
to dare and a discriminating taste make the city a magnet for
inventive chefs and a haven for adventurous eaters—whether in a
five-star restaurant, in the latest ethnic lunch counter, or curbside
at a pushcart.

## ■ They Make Bagels the Old-fashioned Way

**Ask just about anyone to name the quintessential New York food,** and
the answer almost invariably will be the bagel. Bagels have swept the

nation. They are as common in the Upper Peninsula of
Michigan as on the Upper West Side of Manhattan, as
available in Boston and Bakersfield as in the Bronx.
Today's bagel is as American as apple pie and quickly
becoming a global success story, New York's culinary
contribution to the world.

Purists would disagree. Not with the contention
that bagel-eating has become nearly universal. No,
what has the true bagelistas up in arms is the idea
that the bagels you buy in Bakersfield or Bombay are
anything like real bagels.

Real bagels, real bagel-eaters will tell you, are not
stamped out by the equivalent of cookie-cutter
machines or steam baked. They must be hand-rolled,
boiled, and oven-baked if they are to qualify as real
New York bagels.

But alas! Even in New York, real New York bagels
are hard to find. In fact, as of this writing, only three
bagelmakers still do it the old-fashioned way. One of
them is Steve Ross, the third-generation proprietor of
Coney Island Bialy and Bagel Bakery, suppliers of
bialys and bagels to the New York area for more than

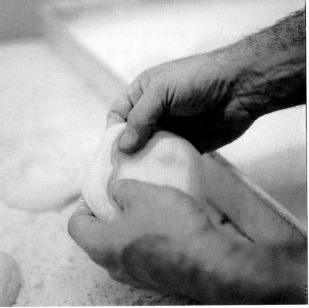

**Real bagels, real bagel-eaters will tell you, are not stamped out by the equivalent of cookie-cutter machines or steam baked. They must be hand-rolled, boiled, and oven-baked if they are to qualify as real New York bagels.**

60 years, during which time nothing about the manufacturing process has changed.

In a neighborhood that once consisted almost exclusively of Jews from Russia and Syria and is now overwhelmingly Asian, the bagel-and-bialy-making process goes on 24 hours a day, with a staff of 15 alternating four shifts. The workers—Italian, Haitian, Puerto Rican, and Brooklyn-born—have all been personally trained by Steve Ross. "It's a dying field," he says. If he wants it done right—and he wants it done right—he has to teach it himself.

The dough mixture for bagels is simple—high gluten flour, New York water (considered a key to the unique taste), fresh yeast, and salt, plus malt.

To make bagels, the baker cuts a strip about an inch and a half by two inches off the dough, rolls the strip by hand, then twists it into a ring to create the distinctive bagel shape. Only handmade bagels display the "lock" that is formed when they are shaped, although skilled bagel-makers twist the dough so deftly that the lock is all but invisible.

It is this, says Ross, this preparing and forming of the dough, that takes so much time and requires so much art. And of course, that is also what makes the taste and texture that bagel purists prize.

Bagel dough takes anywhere from 20 minutes to two hours to rise, depending on the weather and the ingredients. To create the 40 different varieties that Coney Island supplies to its clientele—markets, food suppliers, and retail customers who stop in or shop on the Internet—Ross and his bakers use ingredients ranging from cinnamon and raisins to sun-dried tomatoes and basil.

The shaped, risen bagels are then boiled in a deep vat called the kettle, another distinction from machine-made bagels, which are typically baked with steam.

When the boiled bagels rise to the top of the kettle, that part of the process is finished. The baker places them upside down on a board already coated with, say, sesame or poppy seeds. Bottoms up, they are shoveled into the oven for two or three minutes till they dry on top (the bagel bottom). Then they're flipped and baked through for another seven or eight minutes till done.

"Done" in bagel terms means a crusty, smooth outside shell and a soft chewy inside. Purists consider the machine-made bagels to be a pale imitation of the real thing, nothing more than English muffins with a hole in the middle, sniffs one true bagel fan. Packaged and frozen varieties don't even bear thinking about.

If bagels are everywhere, the bialy is relatively unknown outside the five boroughs. The dough is similar to bagel dough but thinner, with a touch of sugar. Originally made in Bialystok, Poland, its first appearance on America's shores is credited to Morris Rosenweig, progenitor of Coney Island Bialys and Bagels, and grandfather of Steve Ross. Rosenweig was a baker who emigrated to America from Bialystok. In fact, bialys were the first product his bakery turned out, only adding a line of bagels later, in response to their growing popularity. So some might say that the real "quintessential New York food" is—the bialy.

**"Done" in bagel terms means a crusty, smooth outside shell and a soft chewy inside. Purists consider the machine-made bagels to be a pale imitation of the real thing.**

# Dining at Jean Georges:
# What Does It Take to Put the Ultimate in Upscale?

**At Jean Georges restaurant,** housed in one of the city's ubiquitous Trump towers, the sign announcing the restaurant is so small as to be almost invisible. The message is clear: Everyone knows where Jean Georges is. There is no need to shout.

Outside, on the city streets, the wind may be howling or the sun baking. But inside, all is serene, cool marble and honey-colored wood, as the well-dressed diners sit down to their very pricey meals.

Yes, what about those prices? At the restaurant, dinner for two can bump your credit card bill to new heights. There is also a lower-priced, but by no means cheap, café. Is it worth it?

That depends. On how sensitive your palate is, and what you're willing to pay to indulge it.

In a city known for its fussiness when it comes to food, Jean Georges takes culinary discrimination to new heights. The roast pork is not from some run-of-the-mill porker. Jean Georges's pigs are raised especially for the restaurant on a small farm in upstate New York, where they are suckled by mothers whose diet has been heavily laced with apples. Seriously. Gives the meat a subtle fruity flavor.

**In a city known for its fussiness when it comes to food, Jean Georges takes culinary discrimination to new heights.**

The fish on the menu is flown in from Maine, or even Europe, in containers constructed to keep the fresh-caught sea bass or tuna refrigerated, but never allows anything as shocking as bare ice to actually touch its flesh. Every year, local farmers bring their seed catalogs to the restaurant and confer, deciding which *haricots verts,* which baby chives, they will grow for the menu this year. Food suppliers in France track the wild asparagus and rush it to Jean Georges's kitchen.

It all adds up. The restaurant's management says that its biggest expense is the food it serves. After that come the salaries of the people who prepare and serve it, and clean up afterward.

"New Yorkers are the most picky eaters in the world," says Jean-Georges Vongerichten, the architect of all this culinary sumptuousness. And he should know. He has restaurants all over the world: in Las Vegas, the Far East, even in France, the traditional home of haute cuisine.

But it is New Yorkers, their palates trained by access to some of world's best food, their natures inclined to striving, who are the hardest to satisfy.

Vongerichten was born in Alsatian France, and trained in classic cuisine in several multistarred restaurants in France. It was while working as the chef at the very posh Oriental Hotel in Bangkok that he began to develop his taste for the lighter cuisine of the East, with its accent on fresh foods and light sauces made with herbs exotic at the time: lemongrass, chilis, galingale.

As a young chef in the '80s in New York, he began to integrate these foods and these cooking techniques into the classic cuisine. It was a marriage of the right chef at the right time. Diners, their palates jaded by the heavy French sauces and increasingly concerned with staying fit, were delighted with the new tastes, the new lightness. The media noticed, and "fusion cuisine"—a blend of Asian and traditional French—was born.

**Vongerichten is fierce in upholding his standards. You don't keep your place at the top of New York's food chain by letting a garnish dribble, a sauce go flat.**

Vongerichten is a man of medium height, surprisingly slim for someone who is passionate about food. His eyes are an intense blue, and become more blue and more intense when he discusses cooking. He has taken some criticism for meddling with the classic cuisine, but he is more convinced than ever that people want fresh food, expertly but simply prepared.

"There are too many problems in the world," he says. "People want simple. If it's scallops, they want to taste scallops. If it's lobster, it's not hidden under a sauce. Three ingredients on a plate."

Three ingredients, yes, but cooked just so, placed just so. Vongerichten, who conceives and creates the recipes for all his restaurants, is fierce in upholding his standards. You don't keep your place at the top of New York's food chain by letting a garnish dribble, a sauce go flat.

Even with all this lavishing of thought and care, sometimes people just don't go for a recipe he's created. "You can construct the most delicious dish," he says, "and the customers will not order it."

But not to worry. When that happens, something called menu

engineering comes to the rescue. It's about positioning, the verbal presentation of the food. "You're offering"—Jean-Georges gropes for the word—"it's not exactly a dream, but something like it. So the way you describe the food is very important. You can change just a few words, and the next night, it will sell."

Words you cannot say if you want New Yorkers to buy your food: "raw," "butter," "cream"—except for desserts. The good words are anything that implies light, seasonal, fresh. Today's diners want to think they are eating healthfully, even if they're not.

Good menu engineering can make anything, from sweetbreads to chocolate, sound as if it's good for you.

And the one surefire menu best-seller?

"Mashed potatoes," say Vongerichten. "You can sell anything with

**Words you cannot say if you want New Yorkers to buy your food: "raw," "butter," "cream"— except for desserts.**

mashed potatoes. People just like them. Maybe, if they don't come here very often, they say to themselves, well, what could he do to mashed potatoes?"

One wonders what happens to the leftovers, the food that isn't sold, in restaurants like Jean Georges, which put such a premium on freshness. The answer is that, barring the occasional gaffe, there are not many leftovers to deal with. Reservations for tables are made days, even weeks, in advance, so there is no mystery about how many people will need to be fed. Every few days the chef de cuisine, the chef in charge of ordering supplies, is given a computer printout telling him how many "covers"—restaurant lingo for the number of people to be served—he will have to produce each day. The computer also tells him the relative popularity of each dish on the menu in the previous weeks.

Based on that, he will project how many lamb dishes he'll need, how many black trumpet mushrooms, and so on.

Because each dish is prepared individually, "à la minute," there are no leftover cooked meats or vegetables. Meats like lamb or beef are simply kept refrigerated and cooked and served the next day. Fish and chicken, though, must be brought in fresh each day. That's why restaurants are more likely to run out of their fish and poultry dishes before their meats. Faulty forecasting.

Speaking of leftovers, no housewife could be more thrifty at

putting them to use than chefs in high-priced restaurants. As Patrick Gioannini, the general manager of Jean Georges puts it, "We use every part of the animal or the vegetable." If a recipe calls for a fish to be filleted, the bones go into making stock. If the white part of a leek is used in a salad, the green goes into a puree. In the rare cases when food cannot be held over, it is cooked and served to a lucky staff. In an industry with precariously thin profit margins, even at this level, waste not, want not is the motto.

And while no effort is spared to put the best meat, fish, and vegetables before diners, the chefs shop around for the best deals on staples, like salt and sugar.

Gioannini is the general factotum of the restaurant, trained in hotel and restaurant management. Born and raised in Monte Carlo, his accent is vaguely European on most occasions. But it can slip into the most haute Parisian if the situation demands it.

And the situation often demands. Among Gioannini's duties is greeting guests and handling celebrities. Like most upper echelon restaurants, Jean Georges has a special telephone number for celebrities to call for reservations. Even with this special treatment,

**But don't get on Patrick's bad side. It's his job to be
sure the restaurant is run as efficiently and profitably as
possible. One way to irk him is to make reservations
and then consistently not show up, without even a call.**

though, the rich and famous sometimes have trouble
making up their minds where they want to dine—until
the last minute. That's when they'll breeze into Jean
Georges at, say, 8 p.m. on a Saturday night with a few
friends in tow and say, "Patrick old man, do you have a
table for me?"

Patrick always does.

Although he may sigh a bit as he tells the story later,
to the guest he presents a smile. His rule is to say yes
first, find the solution later.

The French accent deepens. Would Mr. Big and
his guests like to wait at the bar for a few minutes?
Their table will be ready soon.

Then, behind the scenes, chaos. A table is produced
from a stash in a storeroom; linens are conjured. The
room is surveyed. Can another table be squeezed in
somewhere, perhaps something set up in the café?
One way or another, the celebrity is accommodated
graciously, no matter how much effort it takes.

But don't get on Patrick's bad side. It's his job
to be sure the restaurant is run as efficiently and profitably as possible.
One way to irk him is to make reservations and then consistently not
show up, without even a call.

"No Call, No Show" the computer screen will display when you call
again and give your name. The computer has been tracking you, and it
*knows*. In this case, the reservation-taker is instructed to ask for a credit
card number to guarantee the reservation. The person is informed that
if he doesn't show, his card will be charged a fee. That takes care of most
multiple bookers, those bane of restaurateurs who reserve a table at
several restaurants, then decide the night of the dinner which one they'll
go to.

But such disciplinary tactics are rare at Jean Georges. It is not a
restaurant with attitude. Attitude is out in these less formal times.
The youthful, attractive staff smiles often, even to strangers. And in an
era when, rumor has it, restaurants track the amount of time people
spend at their meals, trying to hustle them out after 90 minutes or so,
Jean-Georges Vongerichten says that will never happen at his place.

"There are people who want to eat quickly," he says. "You can tell
who they are. They order fast and they eat fast. There are other people

who are here, maybe for a special occasion, and they want to stay for a while."

Either way, it's all right with him. "This is a business about sensing people's needs," he says. "It's about pampering the people. If you don't like to pamper people, you shouldn't be doing this. You should go become a broker or something."

## A Kosher Meals-on-Wheels

**If you're old and frail and poor in New York,** it isn't difficult to find meals-on-wheels services providing hot food and balanced nutrition. If you're old and frail and poor, and a religious Jew who "keeps kosher," it's a bit more complicated.

To "keep kosher," you must follow strict dietary laws that govern both the kinds of food that may be eaten and the way it is prepared. You must shop in special sections of the supermarket, cook foods in a rigorously prescribed manner, maintain two sets of dishes and silverware so as not to mix meat meals and dairy meals. And because you may not cook on the Sabbath, which runs from Friday sundown to Saturday sundown, you must prepare a meal Friday afternoon that can simmer on the stove through the next day.

Even for people who have kept kosher all their lives, doing so in old age can be burdensome.

But here comes Steve DeLorenzo bringing kosher meals-on-wheels—"food and friendship," it says on the side of the van—to the homebound Jewish elderly of New York. Steve and the meals come from Dorot, a social services organization whose mission is to enhance the lives of Jewish and other elderly in the city and "to foster mutually beneficial interaction between the generations." Dorot is Hebrew for generations.

Every Monday and Tuesday, Steve starts his day at around five thirty in the morning, in a food warehouse in Queens where he bags the

**Steve dispenses more than food. He changes a lot of lightbulbs and batteries. At special holidays, he uncorks wine bottles that elderly, arthritic fingers cannot manage. And he listens. He talks. He tells jokes.**

Bringing food and friendship to the

frozen meals ordered two weeks in advance by each of the 100 or so clients he serves. Seven meal choices are offered every week, all certified by rabbinic authorities as "glatt kosher." That's actually a technical term having to do with the condition of certain internal organs in animals, but it has come to mean kosher to the nth degree.

It takes a couple of hours to bag the orders, pack them into insulated bags, and stack the bags in the back of the Econoline van, arranged in sequence for delivery. By 9 a.m., Steve is in Manhattan, making his first stop of the day. On Thursdays, he does it all again— this time for the shabbos meals that can be defrosted on Friday to last through the Sabbath.

Steve dispenses more than food. He changes a lot of lightbulbs and batteries. At special holidays, he uncorks wine bottles that elderly, arthritic fingers cannot manage. And he listens. He talks. He tells jokes. (He is, of course, an actor in his spare time.) He chats with the home healthcare attendants. He parries requests that he stay and have a cup of tea. "They want company," he says. "They want to know what I'm doing 'later.'"

Ninety-nine percent of the people to whom he delivers, by Steve's estimate, are gracious, grateful, even engaging. But being old and weak and sick makes some people ill-tempered—even ill-mannered— and sometimes, they take it out on the man bringing them food and friendship. Steve is the son of an Italian father and a Puerto Rican mother and was raised a Protestant, but when he is the object of an old Jewish lady's crankiness, "it's like being yelled at by my grandmother."

## ■ Why New York Makes the Best Smoked Fish

**A New Yorker who moved to the Midwest** was puzzled by the fact that the smoked fish she bought in her new hometown tasted nothing like the smoked fish she had eaten all her life in New York. Her puzzlement increased when, questioning both her local smoked-fish dealer and her old New York fish merchants, she learned that in both places, the provenance of the fish was the same—the Great Lakes for most whitefish, the Atlantic and some Northwest waters for the salmon. Why then did the New York smoked fish look, taste, and feel so different—in her perhaps biased eyes, so much better—than in her adopted city?

The difference, she learned, was in the smoking process itself. It's in the woodchip mixture for smoking the fish, the very air used to keep the fish cold and to fan-dry it between curing and smoking, certainly the water to create the brine and rinse the fish, and perhaps above all, the art of the smoker—the expert knowledge and sheer instinct that

determine the right moment to dry this batch, the moment to apply the smoke, the moment to stop the process.

And the fact is that the smokehouses of New York have been turning out fine smoked-fish products for a very long time—at least since the late 1800s and early 1900s when more than a million East European Jews settled in New York, bringing with them a culture and cuisine that prized smoked fish.

In an industrial Brooklyn neighborhood that is just beginning to gentrify around the edges sits the descendant of one of those early smokehouses. It is the Acme Smoked Fish Corporation—50,000 spotlessly clean square feet of curing tanks, smoking ovens, slicing and stuffing and packing machines. Acme processes some 10,000 to 15,000 pounds of salmon daily, about a million pounds a year. It

hot-smokes anywhere from 3000 to 5000 pounds of whitefish per day.

All that fresh fish from the Great Lakes or Atlantic waters is loaded onto refrigerated trucks that drive straight through to Brooklyn, pulling into the Acme loading dock anytime around the clock any day except Saturday. The fish is quickly gutted and cleaned and just as quickly moved to the holding rooms, perennially at 36 degrees F. Workers in rubber boots, rubber gloves, and the necessary warm clothes under aprons and smocks move racks of fish along the corridors, which other workers seem constantly to be cleaning.

Salmon and tuna are cured for anywhere from a few days to seven or eight—depending on the type of fish, size, and texture. Whitefish cures for one or two days. To make the different brines that cure the different fish, salt is liquefied into a 100-percent solution, and brown sugar is added. That basic solution is then modified to create precisely the right recipe for the right fish.

Salmon and tuna are then cold-smoked, at a temperature of some 70 degrees. The smoke from a mix of hardwood chips, kept moist to smolder, not burn, is powered through pipes into the vast, two-story brick smoking room. Whitefish is hot-smoked for several hours in smaller steel ovens.

While computers monitor and control much of the process, the "art of it," says operations manager Richie Schiff, is "knowing when to apply the smoke." That is why Acme's smokers are in and out of the ovens, touching, testing, assessing until they judge that the moment is right. "If you smoke it at the wrong time," says Schiff, "the whitefish skin won't be that rich golden color."

Mostly, Acme supplies what some New Yorkers still call "appetizing stores"—although many are now known as high-end gourmet markets—as well as food service distributors, hotels, and supermarkets. Fourteen trucks take Acme's smoked fish as far north as Massachusetts and as far south as Delaware. Common carriers and air shipments take it all over the country, where presumably, people taste the difference.

**Amparo Salazar makes tortillas. Period. She makes them by hand. It is all that she does, and she does it all day long, day after day.**

**Acme's smokers are in and out of the ovens, touching, testing, assessing until they judge that the moment is right. "If you smoke it at the wrong time," says Schiff, "the whitefish skin won't be that rich golden color."**

"Some say it's the Brooklyn water," Richie Schiff suggests. Whatever makes the difference, Schiff, pointing to a slab of Acme's smoked salmon, is convinced that fish smoked elsewhere "isn't this." A New Yorker living in the Midwest would agree.

## Handmade Mexican Tortillas in Manhattan

**In the often frenetic world** of a restaurant kitchen, specialties abound. There are chefs, executive chefs, sous-chefs, and expediters, each with their own well-defined turf. There are line cooks who cook only fish or only meat or only vegetables, others who only sauté or only grill.

And then there is Amparo Salazar.

At Gabriela's Mexican restaurant on Manhattan's Upper West Side, Amparo Salazar makes tortillas. Period. She makes them by hand. It is all that she does, and she does it all day long, day after day. Gabriela's has been in business on Amsterdam Avenue at 93rd Street since 1995. So has Amparo.

But she has been making tortillas since 1968. She was a little girl then, living in Tlapa in the

39

On a typical day, she'll create nearly 20 pounds of dough—a large armful that rides high out of the metal bowl it's mixed in, looking more like a bulging pale yellow stone than the start of a thousand meals.

Sierra Madre del Sur in the state of Guerrero, about a hundred miles from Acapulco. Back then, every step of the process was by hand. Today, the technology has advanced: Amparo uses a simple metal handpress to stamp out the round tortilla shape.

For a normal weekday's quotient of tortillas, she starts making dough in the morning, blending corn mix and water. On a typical day, she'll create nearly 20 pounds of dough— a large armful that rides high out of the metal bowl it's mixed in, looking more like a bulging pale yellow stone than the start of a thousand meals.

Amparo grabs a handful of the dough and rolls it into a ball between her hands. Now another. And another. When there is a pile of balls, like a pyramid of ammunition for a small cannon, she takes one and begins to slap it flat.

Slap. She pulls at it, stretching the dough out, rolls it up again, slaps it again. Push. Pull. Smack—until finally it is ready to be set on the bed of the press.

The bed is lined with a wafer-thin piece of virtually transparent plastic. Amparo puts another piece of wafer-thin plastic on top of the dough, closes the handpress, presses, then lifts the top. She peels the plastic away from the tortilla and parks it on a griddle, which she has earlier sprinkled with vegetable oil. It takes about two minutes for the tortilla to cook. During those two minutes, Amparo takes another ball of dough, slaps it flat, presses it, until the piles of finished tortillas rise in stacks around her.

The result is some 500 tortillas. When those 500 are ready, Amparo starts on another 20 pounds of dough.

That's on weekdays. On weekends, she'll go through the process as many as four times.

There's a good reason Gabriela's employs Amparo. Prepackaged tortillas, made on huge machines, break when folded, feel like rubber, taste like cardboard. Amparo's tortillas, used also for enchiladas and tacos, are light, fluffy, and enfold food easily. "The difference is total," says restaurant manager Jose Zubiaur. He's right. You can taste it.

**Amparo's tortillas, used also for enchiladas and tacos, are light, fluffy, and enfold food easily. "The difference is total," says restaurant manager Jose Zubiaur. He's right. You can taste it.**

*In New York, where everything is bigger than life, it seems that more people work at unusual jobs, and the jobs they work at are more unusual.*

# New York Works— At the Strangest Jobs

**P**EOPLE WORK AT ODD AND UNUSUAL JOBS in every city and town in the country. But in New York, where everything is bigger than life, it seems that more people work at unusual jobs, and the jobs they work at are more unusual. The city's very diversity makes it open to all kinds of occupations, just as it is open to all kinds of languages, foods, and artistic endeavors. For the ways people find to make a living, as for the ways people choose to live, in New York, almost anything goes.

## Honeybees Buzz on a Manhattan Rooftop

**David Graves was worried about his queen bee.** Her brood, the still unhatched larvae that had developed from her eggs, was pretty sparse. Graves decided he would come back in the evening with a new swarm of bees to supplement the current colony—and with a new queen that could lay more eggs and build up the population of his hive.

The hive in question is on the roof of a building some 12 stories above Manhattan. It's one of 17 hives Graves keeps in the city. The

hives are the source of the New York City Rooftop Honey this Massachusetts farmer sells at city green markets, at the family country store, and on his Internet Web site. And it sells very well. New York honey is unusually sweet, sweeter than, say, honey from Vermont or New Jersey.

The honey supplements the other items in the Graves family line of products: jams and jellies made to Mary Graves's recipes from handpicked berries and fruits, and maple syrup made from the family's own maples in the Berkshire Mountains near Becket, Massachusetts.

As it turns out, New York is a great place for honeybees. For one thing, there are no bears in the city. Not yet, anyway. The Berkshires are full of black bears, and black bears love honeybee broods, so the Graveses were always struggling to place their Massachusetts hives as high up as possible. In New York City, you can put a beehive well out of reach of any bear just by taking the elevator.

This particular hive is almost out of reach of Graves himself. It is set on an inaccessible corner of roof that Graves gets to by shimmying across a pipe. From up here, you can see why bees would thrive in the city. A nearby high-rise apartment building appears as a wall of terraces, each festooned with flower boxes, hanging plants, and tubs full of early spring blooms. Smaller tenements have window boxes at almost every window. A couple of penthouses have turned their rooftops into virtual forests.

But while rooftop gardens are nice, Graves says it is the flowering trees in the city's parks and community gardens that are the real sources of pollen and nectar for the bees. Graves's hives are all in Manhattan, but bees can fly as far as three miles. So the bees can forage over a varied arboreal range—and they can sip from a number of waterways as well. They like linden trees, and the honey that results from that preference has a hint of mint. Then there are sumac, locust, clover, and all the flowering fruit trees that grow in the parks and along Manhattan's side streets.

**As it turns out, New York is a great place for honeybees. For one thing, there are no bears in the city. Not yet, anyway.**

Now a full-time enterprise, the Graves family business, Berkshire Berries, started as a sideline at weekend green markets. One of them was the Union Square Greenmarket just north of Greenwich Village. All those rooftops proved alluring, and in 1997, Graves established his first city hive. To find other locations, he placed a sign on his green-market table. It read: "We're very gentle, and we'd like to share our honey. Do you have a rooftop?"

43

People were intrigued. Many, says Graves, hoped to teach their children something about farming in general and beekeeping in particular. Others were eager to gain the benefit of immunity to local allergies that locally produced honey is said to provide. So many people persuaded their landlords to allow hives that Graves was overwhelmed with offers.

His current complement of 17 high-rise hives runs from the Upper West Side to the Lower East Side. He typically averages about 80 pounds of honey a year from a hive. His record was 140 pounds from one hive on an Upper West Side rooftop. Proving again that there's more sweetness in New York than most people suspect.

## Making Artificial Eyes: It's a Delicate Business

**Henry Gougelmann is part of a select group**. He's an ocularist, a person who makes and fits artificial eyes. Gougelmann estimates there are only about 100 ocularists in the entire nation.

He himself has been at it since 1950. For a while in college, he thought about going into the priesthood, but the lure of the family business won out. Henry became the third generation of Gougelmanns to head the business founded by his grandfather.

In fact, Peter Gougelmann, Henry's grandfather, introduced custom-made and custom-fitted glass eyes to America. Until he arrived here, in the mid-19th century, people had to settle for stock items imported from Europe, which fitted poorly and may or may not have matched the natural eye.

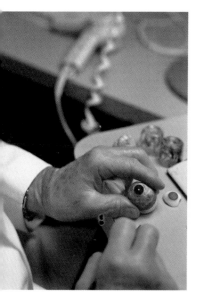

Glass eyes, or ocular prostheses, as they are properly called, are no longer made of glass. That went out in the '50s. Today, they are constructed of a medical-grade acrylic plastic, polymethyl methacrylate—PMMA, that can be fitted to an impression and re-molded for adjustment. PMMA is also more durable than glass and enhances motility, where that is possible.

Entering one of the patient rooms in Mager & Gougelmann's East Side office feels more like stepping into a small artist's studio. A palette contains daubs of paint that have clearly just been squeezed out of a tube. There are brushes, tiny inkwells filled with clear liquids, and

**Glass eyes, or ocular prostheses, as they are properly called, are no longer made of glass. That went out in the '50s. Today, they are constructed of a medical-grade acrylic plastic.**

magnifying lights for close, highly detailed work. The artist image is apt, for artistic aptitude is as necessary to an ocularist as scientific savvy and technical know-how. So are psychological skill, aesthetic sensibility, and a reassuring manner.

People lose an eye or lack one because of accidents, some congenital condition, or because they have suffered a disease that has damaged or destroyed their eye. The choice of prosthesis starts with an assessment of the physical situation—how much of the original eye and surrounding anatomy is intact—then an analysis of other factors: the psychological status of the patient, the potential for side effects or infection. In many cases, a complete globe is not needed. Perhaps a blind person wants to improve the look of his unseeing eye. That person might want only a cover shell over the natural eye. Actors, too, may seek cover shells for theatrical effect.

Whatever the issues, the aims, says Henry Gougelmann, are the patient's comfort, the motility of the prosthesis, and an aesthetically pleasing result.

To make the eye, Gougelmann first takes an impression of the socket. This is a lot like a dentist's taking an impression of teeth. He injects an alginate that becomes rubbery in minutes. From the impression, "we make a mold," Gougelmann says, then embed polymethyl methacrylate into the mold to create the individual shape, which can be adjusted and modified to get the contours just right.

Once the right shape is achieved, outlining as closely as possible the shape of the lid and the size of the opening, it's time to paint the eye.

This is delicate work. Imagine trying to paint, onto a small spherical shape, the exact match of your own eye. The white of the PMMA serves for the sclera—the white of the eye, the tough, fibrous tissue that covers the eyeball. Gougelmann then sets a black disk on a toadstool of putty, just to hold it in place, and begins to paint the iris. He'll typically use three different colors—one for the collarette around the pupil, one for the main eye color of the iris, and one for the limbus, the edge between the iris and the sclera. For bloodshot eyes, Gougelmann uses red-pigmented silk or rayon thread, setting it in a pattern that matches the bloodshot look of the other eye. Clear plastic is placed over the finished work to seal the painting, and the work is done. With care, an ocular prosthesis should last for several years.

**This is delicate work. Imagine trying to paint, onto a small spherical shape, the exact match of your own eye.**

Henry Gougelmann has worked with people from every walk of life. He has worked with babies as young as five days old, with the very easygoing, and with individuals whose lives have been shattered by the loss of an eye. Among the firm's many satisfied clients are such celebrities as actors Paul Muni and Peter Falk and Senator Thomas Gore, Al's father. Henry's two sons are ocularists, too, like their father and grandfather and great-grandfather before them. It's a family calling.

## ■ She Talks to Animals, and They Talk Back

**Is your kitty off its feed?** Or has your formerly docile doggie turned into Conan the Barbarian? Check with a vet, by all means. But you might also want to enlist the services of an animal communicator.

Animal communicator? Yes—although the more precise term may be interspecies communication specialists, individuals who claim to be gifted and trained to enter into dialogue with animals. So explains Rae Ramsey.

A charming, stylish woman, Ramsey lives with her husband on Manhattan's Upper East Side. And she has turned her gift for communicating with animals into a livelihood. According to Ramsey, her communication is based on the belief that direct telepathy between humans and animals is possible. Certainly, animals communicate in the obvious ways: through body language, meows, and barks. Telepathy, however, goes beneath the obvious. It reveals the underlying causes of behavior and can elicit answers to specific questions.

Ramsey believes we all have telepathic ability, but that in most of us, it has become dormant with disuse. In her case, the "tremendous intuition" she has always possessed combined with her love of, as she says, "everything creeping, crawling, or going around on four or more legs," made her able to communicate with animals even as a child. "I was always talking to animals, and I always felt I knew how they felt. But of course, after a while, I stopped talking about it. It's not the sort of thing that necessarily goes down well when you're a teenager trying to fit in."

Instead, Ramsey became a singer of opera and oratorio—about as direct a form of communication, telepathic or otherwise, as you can find. She also became a communications coach, and she studied such holistic healing techniques as Reiki and Therapeutic Touch. In due course, she undertook formal animal communication studies and set up shop in a corner of her bedroom.

A client calls. Maybe someone's dog has suddenly and inexplicably begun to act out. Perhaps it's a family whose animal companion—Ramsey dislikes the word pet—has been diagnosed with a terminal illness. Ramsey and the client make an appointment, and Rae asks for a photo of the animal to be sent to her ahead of time.

At the appointed time, Ramsey awaits the client's call. She's at her desk, telephone headset on and ready. First, she takes down basic information: breed, age, gender. Then the client hears only silence.

**At the appointed time, Ramsey awaits the client's call. She's at her desk, telephone headset on and ready. First, she takes down basic information: breed, age, gender. Then the client hears only silence.**

The animal may be anywhere—in the room, outside, asleep. Ramsey is staring at the animal's photo. She closes her eyes to let her mind's eye take over, focuses on the animal's essence. Telepathically, she asks the animal's agreement to have the conversation. No animal has ever said no.

Then she fills the animal in on what the human client is concerned about. She defines an issue to the animal by picturing the situation. For the terminally ill dog, she might envisage the animal lying on a table in the vet's office, then at home. In a sense, she's asking the dog where it wants to die. Or her mind's eye will picture the animal doing the thing the human client wants done. She might visualize two sparring cats getting along better, for example.

Communication from the animal arrives as well. It may be the image of a fully formed thought. Or sometimes Ramsey feels it as a bodily sensation—a temperature change, or a tingling reaction. And while hunches and feelings may be part of what she senses, she is certain that she is engaged in a conversation with the animal.

"We don't really know how it works," she says, "but I am actually getting information from the animal."

For Ramsey's human clients, knowing the feelings of their animal companions is cheering, enriching, and worth paying for. And she points to many successes. There was a bereaved dog, who, after the death of his master, kept rolling around in a pond, emerging muddy and dirty. The dog's owner, also bereaved, enlisted Ramsey's help. When she "spoke" with the dog, she says, she felt so much grief she was reduced to tears herself.

The dog felt he had a double loss. He'd not only lost his master, his mistress, grief-stricken at the loss of her husband, had retreated into herself and was ignoring her dog. His solution: the soothing muddy waters of the pond.

Ramsey negotiated a deal with dog and mistress. The dog would spend less time in the pond if the mistress spent more time with him. So far, it seems to be working.

And there are others; for example, the snooty cats who refused to take orders from the bossy Australian sheepdog in the family. With Ramsey as mediator, the cats agreed to take some "suggestions" and the dog agreed to accept rejections in good grace.

Then there was the promiscuous dog who would follow any friendly face home, forcing his mistress out in the night to find him. Ramsey negotiated some rules; the dog could visit some places, but not others. So far, she says, he's a lot better, though not completely cured.

As to the skeptics, Rae Ramsey remains unruffled and composed. "The proof of this work is in the benefits," she says. When the cat spats stop, Ramsey and her clients know it's working.

**Telepathically, she asks the animal's agreement to have the conversation. No animal has ever said no.**

## ■ Flyerman—He'll Post Your Posters

**New York is a world center of advertising.** But that's of little use to someone who has something for sale but not the capital for getting the word out. If you lack the hefty means for a television or radio spot or even a few lines in a newspaper, how can you get yourself on the map in the marketplace of New York?

Enter Martin the Flyerman. He'll post your flyer on bulletin boards and storefronts in any neighborhood you choose, or across the city for that matter.

Why Martin the Flyerman? Why not just paste up the ads yourself? After all, you can buy Scotch tape, too.

Ah. But where will you put them? You can't just paste up a flyer willy-nilly in New York. For one thing, it's a violation to post flyers on any city property. For another, store owners and building residents have become sensitive to the disorder that a lot of flyers tacked up

**From decades-long experience, he knows where flyers can and cannot be posted. Tell him which neighborhood or districts you want covered, and he'll hop on his bike, knapsack full of flyers on his back, and off he goes.**

messily can present, especially when the tackers are competitors who have no compunction about tearing off one another's flyers.

That's where Martin comes in. From decades-long experience, he knows where flyers can and cannot be posted. Tell him which neighborhood or districts you want covered, and he'll hop on his bike, knapsack full of flyers on his back, and off he goes. Martin knows which delis allow displays. He knows the shops, photocopy centers, cleaners, and Laundromats, supermarket entryways, church halls, even college campuses where bulletin boards allow for this cheap but effective form of publicity.

And there is more. He also knows which bulletin boards take down flyers on which dates —some on the first of the month, some on the fifteenth. And he's friendly with enough building doormen to have entry to a number of promising basement laundry-room bulletin boards.

Martin never dissembles about his purpose; he never violates city laws or building-specific regulations. He is absolutely aboveboard about what he is doing. And because everyone in New York knows that flyers are an essential means of communication, he is allowed into areas that would likely be off-limits to others.

The Flyerman's clients are people with a service to sell, an organization to push, an event to announce, a house or apartment to sublet. They include a chiropractor, lots of computer consultants, actors, apartment and closet organizers, people looking for space to rent, and people with space looking for renters. Most of the flyers are the typical New York style, with a fringe of phone numbers so that anyone interested can pull the number off the flyer and pocket it. Some are simple, words typed on a plain piece of paper. Others are elaborate computer-generated designs in a snappy typeface with a catchy graphic on brightly colored stock.

Martin says the look of the flyer has a lot to do with how effective his work is. He tells his clients that results will take time. Putting up a flyer is not magic, which is why he makes no promises. Yet he is convinced that eventually flyers work. One client, in fact, says that Flyerman's services are as effective as placing an ad in the Yellow Pages, and far more cost-effective.

When potential clients ask how they can be sure he's posted their flyers, Martin turns the tables and asks them where they saw his flyer. (Of course, Martin advertises his own service by flyer, too.) Invariably, the answer to his question is, "Everywhere." That, he assures them, is the payoff they're looking for.

## A Doll Hospital: Tiny Patients, Big Rewards

**Grown women—grandmothers!—**have been known to grow misty-eyed when they recall how their childhood dolls were given new life at the New York Doll Hospital: a torn limb on a golden-haired beauty repaired, a teddy bear's eyes replaced. One woman recalls a French doll her mother brought her from the Paris flea market in the 1950s, when she was eight or nine years old. It had a wooden, articulated body and a porcelain head. Dressed in a beautiful white dress and dark green velvet coat, it was a little princess of a doll.

**The work done in this cluttered, musty aerie is absolutely meticulous, painstaking. It also requires an aesthetic sensibility and some sense of the whimsical.**

This was a brunette princess, with shiny curly hair—which the little girl promptly cut, and instantly regretted doing. Her mother took her and the doll to the New York Doll Hospital, where the experts of the Chais family provided a beautiful new head of hair. Little girl and doll lived happily ever after.

Irving Chais, the third member of his family to own and operate the business, has "no competition—none whatever in the United States," he says. Anytime and anywhere this specialized work is needed, it flows to the New York Doll Hospital, leaving Chais and his associate, Luis, working on up to 40 dolls at a time.

The Chais family's presence on the second floor of a building on Lexington Avenue dates back to 1898, when Irving's grandparents managed a beauty parlor in the two-room suite overlooking the avenue. Dolls' wigs were a sideline of the beauty parlor. But in a period in which dolls were handmade and highly prized, and much too precious for children to play with, the sideline soon became the main business. In 1900, they turned the beauty parlor into the New York Doll Hospital; it has been here ever since.

The work done in this cluttered, musty aerie is absolutely meticulous, painstaking. It also requires an aesthetic sensibility and some sense of the whimsical. One must combine the miniaturist diligence of a watchmaker with the creativity of an artist. And it cannot be rushed. Repairs or restoration on a valuable antique doll can take months and cost thousands of dollars.

The hospital's two rooms—a bit threadbare in a Dickensian way— are filled with "anything related to dolls," as Chais breezily describes the contents. In shelves lining the walls of the front room are dolls of every imaginable type. Here are ventriloquists' dummies, Barbies, Alice in Wonderland, Raggedy Anns, precious antiques, dolls of many lands dressed in their ethnic costumes. There are 1950s Japanese dolls that run on two batteries—a hot collectible, says Chais—headless torsos and bodiless heads.

Chais buys parts from everywhere, and he travels all over the city to find the right materials to use in his work—just the right paints to create flesh tones and rosy cheeks, just the right lacquer for repairing porcelain, very fine red sable brushes, imported from France, to do such detailed work as eyebrows.

**There are special tools for poking inside a porcelain head to pluck out the eyes.**

There are special tools for poking inside a porcelain head to pluck out the eyes, special mild soaps for washing porcelain without damaging the paint. Special lacquers, adhesives, candle wax, plaster of Paris. The old original skill—that of the beautician—is another requirement, as Chais and Luis create and apply new wigs, replicating the exact hairstyle of the old wig or creating an entirely new look.

The most valuable doll Chais ever worked on was an ancient Egyptian doll made of gold. The property of a museum, it had suffered a break and was sent to Chais for repair. It was, he says, "thousands of years old," and as to dollar worth, it was simply priceless, irreplaceable and inestimable. Yet repairing it was a simple job, for which Chais in good conscience charged no more than $35.

## ■ Tycoon of the Dog-walkers

**Among dog-walking entrepreneurs in New York,** the competition has become—well, dog-eat-dog. It is not enough these days to simply take a dog for a walk. The dog-walker must provide what the marketing experts call added value, something that sets this dog-walker apart from all other dog-walkers.

New York very likely invented the dog-walker job, as artists, poets, and out-of-work actors turned what is typically a shared family chore into a livelihood, one that left ample time for painting, writing, or

auditioning. And the city almost certainly invented the dog-walking business, through which a onetime dog-walker can aspire to becoming a tycoon—directing squads of dog-walkers across the boroughs, perhaps beyond.

Dog-walking was Cathy Jablow's first job after she finished college and before she knew precisely what she wanted to do with her life. For an animal lover who adores dogs and cats—she has two of the former and five of the latter—it was, in a sense, the perfect job. She was with her preferred creatures. "I can't think of anybody I'd rather be with than dogs," she says. And it paid the bills.

But there were hazards. Winter ice was one. Walking 12 hours a day on hard pavement was another, felt with particular intensity in the knees. Since she had no set route, Jablow circled the city haphazardly, heading first uptown, then downtown, then back uptown, following not logic or efficiency, but the needs of her customers. And even though she loved the animals she took care of, it was a hard way to make a living.

Then came marriage and a brief career as a headhunter in a corporate recruiting firm. Headhunting was a long way from dog-walking, but it would prove to be good training for sizing up potential hires later.

The marriage ended in a difficult divorce, which left Cathy in need of healing and eager, in her words, "to be in the company of God at all moments." To her, that meant animals, not people.

But by this time her entrepreneurial spirit was asserting itself. She would start her own business. Its distinctive differentiators would be the length of the visit (45 minutes), and the fact that dogs are walked individually, so that the family pet feels "attended to" during the day, not possible when a single walker is running ten dogs on leashes. An added attraction is that the walker will groom and play with the animal.

In 1985, Jablow put an ad in *The*

> **She would start her own business. Its distinctive differentiators would be the length of the visit (45 minutes), and the fact that dogs are walked individually, so that the family pet feels "attended to."**

*Village Voice,* advertising for walkers, and launched Pet Patrol, the business she has managed ever since. Now the instrument of her work is not a leash and a set of plastic bags for complying with New York's pooper scooper law, but a Mac computer, on which she juggles schedules and creates routes so her walkers won't have to zigzag around the city, as she once did. She also publishes a newsletter for clients, groomers, vets, and other interested parties.

Pet Patrol's clients are mostly people who work during the day and can't do the two daytime walks dogs should have, in addition to morning and nighttime outings. Some people need a cat-sitting arrangement, which she also handles. In a city where so many keep long working hours, one wonders why they even bother to have an animal. Jablow will tell you it's because most people absolutely love their pets—but also love to work. She will also tell you that for some people a dog is a fashion accessory or, in her phrase, "a chick magnet."

That there is a market for such a service is not in question. At one time, Pet Patrol staffed 14 walkers handling as many as 90 jobs a day and delivering an annual revenue in excess of a quarter-million dollars. It was, in Jablow's words, "too big, almost out of control, vulnerable to mistakes." She made the decision to stay small and streamlined the operation, reemphasizing her original goals: to be involved with animals, to enjoy the freedom of running her own business, to support herself in Manhattan.

Think of Pet Patrol as a specialist boutique in the increasingly big-business world of dog-walking. And for even more added value Jablow does tarot readings—for owners, not animals.

# Doing Business— On Main Street and Wall Street

**W**HEN THE GLOBAL ECONOMY and 24/7 became all the rage, New Yorkers could be excused for laughing up their sleeves. Twenty-four/seven? That's an old story. The city has long bought and sold around the clock, in some 150 languages, in markets of varying shades of black, white, and gray. Business acumen is the city's life-blood. If it exists, you can find it in New York. And if it doesn't exist, New York will find a way to create it and sell it to you.

## What Are Those Water Tanks Doing There?

**They sit at the top of most high-rise buildings** in the city, odd, casklike objects with conical tops, like the straw hats that bob on an Asian peasant, or some forest of strange tepees.

They are the water tanks of the city, and it's difficult to figure out why they stir such affection in the hearts of New Yorkers. Maybe it's their woodenness—cypress, redwood, cedar—in a city of concrete and metal. Maybe they evoke nostalgia for a simpler era, for the tanks themselves are as simple as a barrel—and are constructed almost exactly the same way. Maybe it's just that the tanks are unquestionably a signature of the city, quietly essential to its skyline.

But what are they doing? Surely a city as mechanized, computerized, and automated as New York does not rely on these tanks for water.

But it does.

Andrew Rosenwach, whose company manufactures the tanks, says that if it weren't for the water reserve requirement of a stringent fire code, the tanks would be obsolete. The code requires that every building higher than six stories maintain a reserve of water sufficient to douse a fire up and down however many stories the building contains. The fire protection reserve is over and above what's necessary to keep kitchen faucets and bathroom showerheads flowing. The six-story rule derives

from the fact that the water that flows into New York via aqueducts from its upstate reservoirs, and then into the plumbing of a high-rise, will make it to the sixth floor—more or less—on its own. Above that level, it needs to be pumped. If the pump should go out, the tanks—and gravity—take over. And if you must put a tank up there to meet the water reserve requirement, you might as well use it to feed the building's domestic water system.

The tanks are kept supplied with water through a system almost identical to the way your toilet bowl works. There's a float attached to a bar. When the float falls to a certain level, more water is pumped in, keeping the reserve always at the legal limits. It's simple, and economic.

The simplicity and economy of the solution are what make Andy Rosenwach the fourth generation of Rosenwachs to be in this business, the sole manufacturer of wooden water tanks in the city. Andy's father, Wallace, reinvented the tank-building process a few decades ago, shortening it from three weeks to 10 hours. That neat bit of re-engineering "made the name Rosenwach mean to water tanks what Kleenex means to tissues," says Andy. Yet even Wallace thought that new technologies would make the wooden water tanks obsolete. "In 20 years," Andy recalls his father saying, "our only water tank business

**Surely a city as mechanized, computerized, and automated as New York does not rely on these tanks for water. But it does.**

will be uninstalling them." He was wrong.

In the Greenpoint workshop where the Rosenwach tanks are built, the warm fragrance of wood hangs in the air. Foreman Ken Lewis and his two coworkers, Ivan Suarez and Rin-Lin Chen, can make one average-sized tank a day, as Wallace Rosenwach decreed—some 200 to 300 tanks per year, depending on demand. An average tank is 13 feet in diameter and 12 feet high—enough to hold 10,000 gallons or so of water. Many tanks are smaller, and some are larger. The biggest tank Lewis ever built was 22 feet in diameter.

The manufacturing process is as straightforward as the final product. Rough lumber—mostly yellow cedar from the Pacific Northwest—is machine-molded into measured lengths for the top, bottom, and sides of a tank. A "finished" tank goes out of the shop as a kit—bottom, staves, hoops—that will be assembled by the installation team. Once assembled, the galvanized steel hoops, also measured to fit by machine in the Greenpoint shop,

**An average tank is 13 feet in diameter and 12 feet high— enough to hold 10,000 gallons or so of water. Many tanks are smaller, and some are larger. The biggest tank Lewis ever built was 22 feet in diameter.**

are looped around the tank and tightened by lugs until there's no daylight at the joints. The tank is filled with water, and it swells out against the hoops till it's absolutely watertight.

That's it. It takes a day to take down an old tank and install a new one. After that, the tank will sit on its roof for 20 or 30 years, beautiful, efficient, and simple in a complicated city.

## ■ Change Your Image in Four Easy Steps

**Feeling stuck? Have a sense that you could be *more?*** More beautiful, more charming, more chic? New York is a place where people reinvent themselves every day. And Carolyn Gustafson is one of the people helping them to do it.

Carolyn has been at it formally since she opened for business in 1985, although she says she consulted informally for years before that. A onetime model and actress, a student of protocol, and a woman who likes organizing, she found herself dispensing advice for free when asked by friends and family. She also found herself musing often about how people could change their image. "I'd sit on the bus and look at someone and picture the person with a different hairstyle or wearing a different color or a different style of clothing."

She liked thinking about it, liked seeing the potential that was in different individuals. And she wanted to help people realize that potential. So in 1985, she wrote a business plan, put an ad in a glossy magazine, and got to work.

Her clients, she says, are "people who feel stuck, who feel that they have been through inner changes and need to make outer changes in order to be 'in sync.' Or maybe they need to change the outside to create a space for changes inside. My job is to help them discover who they are and to feel comfortable with who they are."

As stunning and straight-backed as you'd expect of a former cover girl, Carolyn spends the first meeting with a client mostly listening. Her aim is to get an idea of the person's spirit, to understand what arena they're in. The reason for such understanding is basic to Carolyn's philosophy: "People should look like who they are," she insists. "They should feel good about who they are." So the first consultation delivers an analysis of the client's potential best appearance—the best color, physical features, makeup, style, wardrobe—along with advice on how to fiddle with all those factors so the client can become "their best self."

> **Her clients, she says, are "people who feel stuck, who feel that they have been through inner changes and need to make outer changes in order to be 'in sync.'"**

Step two is a wardrobe review. Carolyn literally goes through her client's closets. Her mantra for every item of clothing is that it meet the "four Fs." It must fit perfectly, be flattering, serve a function in the client's life, and be fabulous. If not—fifth F—flunk it!

In step three, Carolyn puts her wardrobe advice into action. She does the legwork for the client's clothes shopping, "preselecting" clothes for the person's new look so all the client has to do is head for the department store and try them on.

Step four is charm school. Carolyn calls it "communication skills coaching" in conversation, body language, even etiquette. In her eyes, it's all based on kindness and respect—plus efficiency. It's the sort of thing corporations like to buy for their rising stars—a way to smooth the rough edges and tame the aggressive manner that made them stars in the first place. Senior managers need to be sure their people aren't shoveling food down their gullets or telling off-color jokes to their dinner companions. So they send them to Carolyn Gustafson.

To her, however, her job is making a difference in people's lives. "When you polish your shoes," she says, "you're not changing the shoes, you're just bringing out the best in them. That's what I help you do for yourself."

## Voice Coach to the Stars— and to You

**Although being a New Yorker** might be a symbol of sophistication, sounding like one is not—at least in some circles. So while Carolyn Gustafson helps people look their best, Elizabeth Dixon helps them sound that way.

"Rounder vowels, please. And don't forget to find the key tonal sound in each word.

"Now bring it down. Softer. And keep as much modulation as you can without losing your sound and without losing your production."

Dixon is directing a voice coaching session for a young woman on the corporate fast track. But if there's anything that can stall the student's upward progress, it's her thick New York accent, the nasal tone of her voice, and the speed with which she talks—faster than a New York minute.

Just about every English speaker in the world can recognize that accent. New Yorkers often lose the *r* that follows a vowel. They say "boid," not "bird." They come to a hard glottal stop in words like "bottle" and tend to explode the *g* sound in words like "long." Even linguists have a hard time describing what New Yorkers do to the vowel in words like "off" or "dog."

New Yorkese is the dialect of tough guys. It's considered low class, uneducated, a metaphor for the rough-and-tumble of slum life. It's something many New Yorkers seek to overcome.

That's when they seek out the likes of Liz Dixon. A onetime actress,

she is the widow of
Alfred Dixon, a renowned
Broadway vocal coach who
helped many actors use
speech to create character.
Dixon had stuttered as a child,
during an era, his widow says, when
stuttering meant "there was something
wrong with your brain. Period. It could never be
fixed." But the young Dixon had dreams of becoming an actor, so
he set about correcting himself. The methods he devised—a body
of exercises for voice conditioning, projection, and expression—
became the basis of the Alfred and Elizabeth Dixon Speech
Systems, which the couple refined and elaborated over the years.

The roster of performers they helped reads like a
theatrical *Who's Who*. Katharine Hepburn, Charles Boyer,
Lauren Bacall, among many, many others. Elizabeth
worked with Margaret Thatcher when she was Prime
Minister of Britain, and helped give speech patterns and a
vocal key to Michael Douglas for his role as the corporate raider

**New Yorkese is the dialect of tough guys.
It's considered low class, uneducated,
a metaphor for the rough-and-tumble of slum life.
It's something many New Yorkers seek to overcome.
That's when they seek out the likes of Liz Dixon.**

in the movie *Wall Street.*

But most of Dixon's clients are not celebrities. They are just folks. Many these days are what she calls "second-language" people—the many immigrants who have brought their talents and ambitions to New York with them. They are perhaps the best exemplars of what Liz Dixon believes vocal coaching can achieve. It can, in her words, release the personality.

"Imagine," says Liz, "that you are a lawyer or a doctor from another country trapped by your inability to be understood." Dixon extends the metaphor to many native speakers who mumble or splutter or gabble or swallow

their words—people whose voices cannot project, or who will not let themselves be heard, or whose every other sound is a hesitant "um" or "like" as they search for the right way to say what they want to say.

Liz Dixon is an evangelist for the ability of speech and voice to change lives. She begins with the premise that the way you speak tells people a lot about you. If "your voice is your invisible calling card," she asserts, "then a new voice is a new you."

It takes physical conditioning and practice to achieve the best. You build your speaking instrument so that your life experience and intelligence come through the sound of your voice, and your personality and character shine through your delivery. The end result, Dixon asserts, is to unleash the person you really are—almost literally to find your voice.

Listen to Elizabeth Dixon and you will believe that. The voice is fresh, belying the idea that achieving the golden-age years gives you a golden-age voice. Dixon's voice resonates. You're aware of a reservoir of power behind it. She speaks with authority. You are drawn into what she is saying. The accent is neutral, yet distinctly American—easy on the ears. When she speaks, you believe what she says.

**Liz Dixon is an evangelist for the ability of speech and voice to change lives. She begins with the premise that the way you speak tells people a lot about you.**

# ■ What Is Behind That Newsstand?

**The corner newsstand is a virtual necessity of city life.** In a place in which nondrivers outnumber drivers, and where going out to do a few errands mostly means going on foot, the newsstand serves as snack bar, rest stop, literary emporium, ticket booth, and possibly the first stop toward winning millions and never having to work another day.

But newsstands are something more. They represent another of those livelihoods, like driving a taxi, that seem tailor-made entry points for immigrants. Recently, that has meant mostly immigrants from the Asian subcontinent.

Surjit Singh has operated a newsstand on Manhattan's posh and busy East Side since 1992—since "March 7, 1992, a Friday," Singh says with exactitude. A native of Ludhiana in the Punjab, in the far north of

**The newsstand serves as snack bar, rest stop, literary emporium, ticket booth, and possibly the first stop toward winning millions and never having to work another day.**

**The biggest seller in this veritable variety store at curbside? Cigarettes—something of a surprise in a city where smoking is pretty much restricted to the streets and the smoker's own living room.**

India, Singh came to the U.S. in 1990. Through the network of Indians already established in New York, he got a job in a Queens candy store. When the network later offered a chance to rent the newsstand, Singh seized the opportunity, and he has been at it ever since.

He opens his stand at about 6:30 a.m.—literally opens it, transforming a sealed box into a cozily enclosed compartment with all products both on display and within reach. The publications come to Singh via the account of the newsstand owner from whom he rents his quasi-franchise, but he orders the food, drinks, and other items from wholesalers on his own account.

The biggest seller in this veritable variety store at curbside? Cigarettes, says Singh—something of a surprise in a city where smoking is pretty much restricted to the streets and the smoker's own living room.

The biggest danger? Kids stealing candy. They come by in packs, says Singh, and despite the Lucite barriers he's constructed, they grab handfuls and run, winding their way through the fashionable pedestrians and quickly disappearing from view.

Behind the barriers and magazines and racks of candy is Singh's personal space, narrow and cramped, but outfitted with a high stool, cashbox, a heater in winter, and a fan in summer. When Singh needs a break, there are "many people" who can mind the store for him—other merchants, the security guard at a nearby building, even waiters from the Indian restaurant across the street, which has the closest bathroom.

He has thus made friends among the people who inhabit, in one way and another, his corner of the East Side, and he has made friends among the regulars who stop by each morning for their newspaper, the joggers who pick up a bottle of water to run with, the stockbrokers who pick up *The Wall Street Journal* every morning and grab a tabloid on their way home, shortly before Singh closes shop just before eight at night, six days a week, and makes his way home to Queens.

**"High price."**

The computer squawks out the message audibly at the same time as the words appear on the screen. SWAT, the Stock Watch Alert Terminal, is doing its job: Signaling the staff of the American Stock Exchange's Stock Watch department that there is unusual activity in a particular stock—in this case, a price out of bounds for this stock at this time.

To the staff of seven whose job it is to monitor the trading floor on a real-time basis, such a "kickout" is hardly unusual. As a matter of policy, the department "errs on the side of caution," in the words of managing director Jay Stewart Bono. All sorts of small anomalies can trigger a kickout: volume fluctuations, price volatility, anything unusual in the trading pattern for a particular stock. SWAT computer monitors line the walls of the small, glass-enclosed Stock Watch department where the seven train their attention on the Exchange's trading activity all day long.

Constant, real-time surveillance is a key element in Wall Street trading. The American Stock Exchange, like most financial exchanges, is a self-regulating organization. Its market surveillance operations are made up of lookouts on the trading floor as well as the computerized eye-in-the-sky stock and options monitoring. Anything flagged by any area of the operation can lead to an investigation and a report that might result in disciplinary action by the Exchange or referral to the Securities and Exchange Commission for investigation and legal action.

"Basically, what we're always looking for," says Bono, "is an appearance of potential insider trading." Bono created the Amex's Stock Watch, and SWAT is his brainchild. It's based on the fact, as Bono describes it, that "there are parameters that are unique to a particular stock,

**The American Stock Exchange, like most financial exchanges, is a self-regulating organization. Its market surveillance operations are made up of lookouts on the trading floor as well as the computerized eye-in-the-sky stock and options monitoring.**

and those parameters are dynamic—that is, they change from hour to hour and from day to day." SWAT is fed those parameters, and carefully calibrated filters operated by complex algorithms kick out the anomaly, the deviation from any parameter. The Amex technology team constantly updates the filters and adds parameters and sharpens the algorithms.

The Amex analyst tracking the company whose high price just triggered a kickout wants to know why the price is on the ascendant. The answer seems to be that earnings are up. So now the analyst wants to know if anybody initiated trading before the earnings were publicly reported. In short, is there anything in the stock's trading activity that looks like the stock was "active before the news," as the jargon has it?

In this case, the analyst determines that the stock's activity is not unusual enough to call a halt to the trading, although halts are much more common than people might think. In fact, Bono says there are "probably two halts per day on average, each lasting maybe two hours."

Stock Watch analysts also routinely monitor corporate disclosures, market reports, and news from the world of trading and finance. They check to see if press releases "seem to excite rather than inform," says Bono, adding that Stock Watch staff are trained to read between the lines. In addition, the staff is plugged into news and financial data from a slew of sources—Bloomberg, NewsEDGE, TrackDATA, and more—giving the staff the ability to initiate off-line inquiries—what Bono calls a "real-time, on-the-fly clipping service."

The analysts monitor any kickout situation throughout the day, and by the end of the day they decide whether or not to send the lead on to the Surveillance and Listed Company Liaison, the SLCL, Rudy Prescod, for further investigation.

That, says Bono, is the main end product of Stock Watch's work, to give leads to the SLCL, to "send it up to Rudy." Rudy's job, in turn, is to decide if the investigation should go even higher. Bono estimates that Stock Watch takes "a hard look" at some 50 kickouts a day, then filters that down to anywhere from five to nine cases that need further investigation or surveillance. And if a stock goes up enough, they refer it anyway, even if no wrongdoing is suspected.

They've caught some big ones. A chance conversation at the water-cooler enabled two analysts to find similar patterns in cases each was studying. The result was the revelation of a major insider trading scam, the one loosely depicted in the movie *Wall Street*. Of course, it's a system whose efficacy is measured only in its successes. When people get away with something, by definition, no one knows about it. It's Stock Watch's job to make sure that doesn't happen.

**They've caught some big ones. A chance conversation at the water-cooler enabled two analysts to find similar patterns in cases each was studying. The result was the revelation of a major insider trading scam.**

# A Coffee Vendor, Complying with City Rules, and with Allah's

**Ibraham Fereig is among the newest** of the city's new entrepreneurs. Ibraham rents a coffee wagon and its curbside space on a busy street corner in Manhattan. He rents the wagon and its space from another entrepreneur further up the business chain, a countryman who started out like Ibraham, with one wagon, but now rents three—subletting them out to people like Ibraham. The rent-sublet process spirals all the way up the entrepreneurial chain. Ibraham doesn't know who, ultimately, owns the cart he rents. But Ibraham's cart is licensed by the city's departments of Health and Consumer Affairs. And it's Ibraham's job to make sure he's up-to-date on his permits and that he complies with a raft of city regulations.

New York's coffee wagons are typically located strategically near a subway station, bus stop, or cluster of office buildings—anywhere large numbers of workers pass by, and Ibraham's is no exception. He works a long day. He starts at two in the morning, traveling from his home in Queens to the coffee wagon depot not too far away in Astoria. Then it's prep time: Fereig picks up his order of bagels, muffins, doughnuts, cold drinks, teas, hot chocolate mix, decaf, and the four gallons of milk and seven pounds of coffee he uses daily. He checks his supplies: cups, lids, napkins, paper bags. Then a friend whose car has a hitch picks him up and takes Fereig and the wagon into Manhattan.

He's in his place by 4:30 or 5 a.m. He lifts his wagon onto the sidewalk, props up the low end on empty boxes, opens the sides, and gets ready for business.

The first rush arrives at about 6 a.m., a crowd of construction workers from a nearby site. Fereig moves with practiced speed and grace. His motions are choreographed for efficiency, and watching him is like seeing an athlete in action. He reaches up to pull down a

**Fereig moves with practiced speed and grace. His motions are choreographed for efficiency, and watching him is like seeing an athlete in action.**

MOBILE FOOD VENDOR
18330

**GOOD MORNING**

| | SM | MED | LG |
|---|---|---|---|
| COFFEE | 50¢ | 75¢ | 1.00 |
| TEA | 50¢ | 75¢ | 1.00 |
| HOT CHOC | 50¢ | 75¢ | 1.00 |
| SANKA | 50¢ | 75¢ | 1.00 |
| HERB TEA | 75¢ | 1.00 | 1.25 |
| BAGEL | | | 50¢ |
| W/BUTTER | | | 50¢ |
| W/CR CHEESE | | | 1.00 |
| ROLLS | | | 50¢ |
| W/CR.CHEESE | | | 1.00 |
| DONUTS | 50¢ | | 75¢ |
| CROISSANT | | | 1.00 |
| DANISHES | | | 1.00 |
| MUFFINS | | | 1.00 |
| SODAS | | | 1.00 |
| JUICE | | | 1.00 |
| TROPICANA | | | 1.50 |
| SNAPPLE | | | 1.25 |
| WATER | | | 1.00 |
| ICE COFFEE | | | 1.25 |

**HAVE A NICE DAY**

Snapple

**PEPSI**

cup, hoists and pours the milk, pulls the handle on the coffee urn, slaps on the lid, slices the bagel and smears it with butter, stretches down to find a bag—all in what seems a single, seamless move. Customer after customer after customer.

Once the construction crew has been dealt with, there's a lull. At around seven, Fereig gets company—at least in the warm weather. A produce seller sets up his stand, and a couple of Senegalese street merchants put up tables from which they'll sell women's handbags and sunglasses. In this curbside mini-mall, the merchants spell one another; Fereig gets a chance for a bathroom break at a nearby deli while the sunglasses vendor keeps an eye on the wagon and lets potential customers know that Fereig will be right back. At around eight, the next wave of customers surges forward—students at the nearby schools, people on their way to work, taxi drivers grabbing a cup of coffee as they head uptown.

Fereig stays open till noon or one o'clock, when his friend with the hitch comes by to pick him up. Then it's back to the garage to "take everything out and wash my wagon with soap and water." He's back home in Astoria by 2 p.m., and not surprisingly, he goes immediately to sleep.

Ibraham Fereig is from a village near Alexandria in Egypt, and will soon become a U.S. citizen. With any luck, he will shortly have enough saved to rent another wagon, which he, too, will sublet. He likes his job but finds it cold in winter. There's a lot to worry about, too: random inspections by health inspectors, crackdowns by city officials checking compliance with regulations, the occasional nasty customer. But giving people their morning coffee is a friendly thing to do, and most people are courteous. There's lots of street life to observe, and as an observant Muslim, Ibraham can control what he's offering and be certain that it is *halal*—that is, permitted by Muslim law.

Fereig's fare is also varied and tasty—to many locals, a worthy competitor to the Seattle-born coffee shop half a block away, where the cheapest cup of coffee is five times the price of Ibraham's coffee. And where the service is considerably slower.

# New York Banners Fly Round the Nation

**They fly so proudly,** banners 35 feet long, 25 feet wide, standing out brilliantly on the façade of the Metropolitan Museum of Art. NEW CHINESE GALLERIES, they announce. JEWELED ARTS OF INDIA. THE NEW SURREALISM.

Huge logo-bearing flags, raised ceremoniously each morning and lowered just as ceremoniously each evening, are the new signage of major corporations, brandishing their sovereignty from the tops of flagpoles. THE NATION OF VERIZON. THE COUNTRY OF PHARMACIA.

These cloth identifiers have an impact. When the New York Public Library followed the lead of museums in the 1960s and flew banners over their front doors, library use shot up. In Brooklyn, Long Island University brought order to their "campus" of disparate, distant buildings by connecting them with identifying flags, and applications for admissions soared.

The contemporary use of these outsize banners and flags has revolutionized publicity, advertising, promotion, and organizational identity. They're everywhere. They announce one-off events. They proclaim hipness. They fray and tatter through winter storms, only to be replaced by colorful new versions in the spring. And many of them, some say the best, come from New York's Kraus & Sons.

**They're everywhere. They announce one-off events. They proclaim hipness.**

**The women who sew and finish the flags and banners still work on hundred-year-old sewing machines—the new ones aren't as good.**

For their size alone, you'd think these prodigious pennants would be put together in vast spaces by vast machines, produced by a cast of thousands on Brobdingnagian devices located in airplane hangars. In fact, they are made by a crew of seven—two production people and five seamstresses—in modest space (6000 square feet) in a somewhat run-down building on the northern edge of Manhattan's Chelsea district. That is where Kraus & Sons Inc. turns out what was once known as regalia.

The process has come a long way since German immigrant Ignacio Kraus started the company in the early part of this century, producing the embroidered emblems prized by New York's unions, the badges of rank and honor beloved of politicians. Kraus & Sons kept at it, broadening their product line to include flags and banners, till the 1960s, when embroidery gave way to sewing the designs onto such new fabrics as nylon and Dacron. That was the same period that the Met Museum initiated its banner program, giving the trend its first important thrust. The 1976 U.S. bicentennial was another breakthrough, giving a huge boost to the use of flags and banners.

Later, digital design and laser printing made the whole process faster and easier. When artwork was on paper, it might take anywhere from seven to 10 days to transfer a small design to a large banner. With artwork on a disk, it takes minutes. But the women who sew and finish the flags and banners still work on hundred-year-old sewing machines—the new ones aren't as good, according to Paul Schneider, who runs Kraus.

"It's a craft, and it takes experience to get it right," Schneider says. He is the son and grandson of printers, whose best customer was Kraus & Sons. The Schneiders bought the business, Schneider says matter-of-factly, "to keep our best customer." As to experience, both the Kraus production director, Jorge Quinones, and Schneider himself have done nothing else but this their entire lives.

It's still a family business. Not just because Paul Schneider's mother, Mildred, does the books for the company but also because there's a family feeling about the place—the longtime workers on the shop floor, the intimacy of a staff that totals 13, including sales and office people.

Kraus ships its flags and banners all over the country, to theaters and museums, colleges and commercial enterprises. The shop does a lot of historic reproductions—copies of old flags for Colonial Williamsburg, for example.

Recently, they were hired by the Women's Rights National Historical Park to reproduce the original banners for women's suffrage, the banners carried in parades and demonstrations leading up to the granting of women's right to vote in 1920. As they unfurled the design, Mildred Schneider remarked, "I remember these." Kraus had embroidered the originals. It was only fitting they should create the copies.

**Kraus ships its flags and banners all over the country, to theaters and museums, colleges and commercial enterprises.**

# The Fashion of New York

**NEW YORK RIVALS PARIS** as the world center of fashion. Not classic couture fashion, although you can find plenty of that, should the occasion arise. Rather, New York sees itself as the global capital of what's new, what's alternative, what "the street" determines is fashion. The ideas that come to life in this city one year will be worn around the country, sometimes even around the world, in the next year. In fashion, New York is young, trendy—and very very serious about its style.

## ■ They Tell You What Colors You'll Wear

**Port. Old Lace. Petrol. Smudge.** No, we're not talking about old wine. Or what happens when your gas tank overflows. These are the colors of the clothing you buy—and of the shoes, makeup, gloves, etc.—and they were determined nearly two years before you actually went shopping for that new suit or pair of pants.

By whom? Very likely by The Color Box, the grande dame of color forecasters in New York.

Four times a year—in October (for the spring 18 months hence), December (for spring/summer), March (for the fall "transition"), and June (for the fall/winter 18 months down the road)—the colorists and designers and sales consultants of The Color Box tell the fashion industry which colors they should be thinking about and working in.

And the fashion industry listens.

How do the forecasters decide on colors? It's a collective decision into which separate perspectives are mixed, like colors, until it's just

right. The colorists bring to the decision their research, including what's been spotted at the twice-yearly fabric shows in Paris. The designers bring news about fashion trends they've seen: what the silhouette will be in 18 months, which fabrics will loom large. The sales consultants, fingers on the pulse of the marketplace, contribute what they've sensed on the street. Add to the mix instinct, experience, savvy, a sense of the cyclical nature of fashion.

Experience teaches that the process is evolutionary. Fashion doesn't go from navy blue one year to shocking pink the next; it diminishes or builds in subtle increments of tone and hue. Savvy suggests that a major change in silhouette means no major change in color. Even fashionistas can't absorb two radical changes at once.

Pull it all together—the research, the know-how, the gut feelings— and four times a year, the forecast is born.

The medium for each forecast is a notebook that defines and pictures the color stories of the season. They really are stories, too. It isn't enough to say "green." The industry needs a layered account, plot and character for the color. They must see its nuances, how it might work with the silhouette forecast for the season, how to put it into prints and patterns, different types of clothing, the power and beauty possible when it is allied with certain other colors, the dangers of misalliance.

**Four times a year the colorists and designers and sales consultants of The Color Box tell the fashion industry which colors they should be thinking about and working in.**

**Each color is presented in a twist of braid fixed by Velcro to the palette board, just like an artist's palette, but with yarns instead of dabs of paint.**

"Rabat" was one of the color stories for women's wear one recent fall/winter. It defined the pale and neutral tones for that season. A photograph from Morocco of a washed pink sandstone wall cut by a pale blue door epitomized the feel of the story, which was described as "light and shadow bleached by the sun and muted by shades." The palette of colors included tea, iris, lapis, glaze, pistachio, terra-cotta—the light greens and blues and rusts you wore that winter—forecasted for you back in June.

"Tapestry" was another color story that season. Its palettes were natural root colors and soft surfaces and shiny "techno" finishes. You wore them as velvet tones—pomegranate, plume, prunier, trefoil, indigo.

But the forecast doesn't just tell the industry all this. It shows them. Each color—mantle, samovar, plum—is presented in a twist of braid fixed by Velcro to the palette board, just like an artist's palette, but with yarns instead of dabs of paint. The Color Box's subscribers—manufacturers and designers of clothing, fabric, cosmetics, footwear, accessories—play with these braided yarns, trying the colors out, seeing how they work.

One, two, three colors: pull them off, move them around. Shuffle the palettes. Mix up the stories. Maybe Rabat's iris for a print background, Tapestry's prunier for the top tone. Bent over the palette boards of their notebooks, the designers play with hues and tones. Silhouettes and fabrics. Mix and match. And a color season is born.

## ■ Where Those Who Know Go to Trim

**In the universe of fashion,** there are worlds within worlds, each with its own piece of real estate—a particular half block or pair of blocks carved out among the narrow and crowded side streets of the garment district. People in the fashion industry know the geography here, know what's really going on behind the façades of these nondescript, even down-at-the-heels older buildings. One of the trade secrets in the industry is the map in the minds of its participants, who can navigate a path to and within each world.

For fabric, they know to troll 39th and 40th streets, maybe ending up at B&J, where three floors of space—15,000 square feet—house as many as 10,000 different fabrics. When they need a button covered or a new

Monica Lewinsky came here
looking for trim for her handbags.
Betsey Johnson stopped in to look
at flower ribbons.

shoulder pad, they head for Steinlauf & Stoller on West 39th. When it's a question of ribbons, trim, tucking, rickrack, maybe they head for Hyman Handler & Sons on West 39th, with ribbons and trim jammed from floor to ceiling.

Or maybe they go to Mokuba.

This is the shrine of high-end ribbons, laces, trim, fringe, cord, piping, braid, typically $60 to $70 a yard, topping off at $126 per yard for a mohair fur tape. All of it has been designed by Keiko Watanabe, daughter of the President of Tokyo-based Mokuba, chief of design, overseer of every detail in every Mokuba store, in Tokyo, Paris, Barcelona, and now New York.

Into the design center on West 39th Street, Mokuba's biggest store, come manufacturers and designers of ready-to-wear and high fashion, of shoes, handbags, hats, even home decoration. Monica Lewinsky came here looking for trim for her handbags. Betsey Johnson stopped in to look at flower ribbons. People from Ralph Lauren and Calvin Klein are in and out. Passionate sewing hobbyists come here, too.

**Suppose it's a special lace trim you want. You tell that to sales executive Karen Green. She'll lead you to racks filled with spools of different lace designs in a range of delicacy and colors.**

Suppose it's a special lace trim you want. You tell that to sales executive Karen Green. She'll lead you to racks filled with spools of different lace designs in a range of delicacy and colors. You find one you like, but you need it in a narrower width than any of the samples on display. So Karen shows you "the books"—the complete Mokuba catalog. While there are a mere 20,000 samples on view at 39th Street, the books show all of the 43,000 designs available. Chances are you find what you need.

Satin. Grosgrain. Taffeta. Fake fur. Something with Victorian quality. Something avant-garde. The right fringe for bedroom curtains and matching pillows. It's all here, waiting for you. At a price.

**From elegant department stores** on Fifth Avenue to the funky boutiques of Soho, the "look" of New York is very much determined by what's in store windows. Deciding what goes in the window is up to a store's fashion director and/or merchandiser, and the decision process is often a battleground of competing interests, the perennial tug of war between *artiste* and commerce. But creating the window display is the job of a specialist who is expert in design, savvy about merchandising, willing to work long hours, and able to remain calm under pressure.

## Dressing a Window— It's an Art

Like Renee Viola, who has created windows for Ann Taylor, Lord & Taylor, and Liz Claiborne as well as for such boutiques as the upmarket personal care purveyor, Origins, which maintains stores in some of Manhattan's trendiest neighborhoods.

Viola, who works as a freelance, says that the key to a successful window is to remember that "it's advertising, so you have to create some kind of message." Once that's determined, Viola is given a list of the items that have to go in the window. Then she decides how to handle each. It all depends on that message. Is the item just there to be beautiful, or is it meant to be sold?

For each of the Origins products, Viola is given a poster with a photo of the product and some copy. After that, she says, "the rest is mine." She asks herself, "What will make the window 'sing'"—what will fill the window visually to strengthen the message on

One thing that's particularly demanding about creating a window display is that it must look good from both sides— to shoppers within the store and to passersby outside.

the poster? She then comes up with a concept and draws a sketch of the window.

For an Origins product called Salt Rub, for example, the poster copy suggests that taking it into the shower with you is equivalent to a full spa experience. So that's what Viola tries to represent. Her sketch shows all sorts of lovely spa accessories floating toward a bathtub: sisal mitts, loofahs, natural sponges, body brushes, spa slippers, and the like. To implement the sketch, she hot-glued the items to clear vinyl so they would appear to float. Then she hopes customers will float into the stores to buy.

One thing that's particularly demanding about creating a window display is that it must look good from both sides—to shoppers within the store and to passersby outside. Another demanding reality is the time constraint. Every window has "its own schedule," Viola says. Some high-profile windows in large department stores, in fact, change as frequently as every week. But for the person designing or executing the new display, the deadline is always the store's reopening in the morning. The pressure is always on to "get it done by tomorrow," Viola says.

## They Tell You What Styles You'll Wear

**This is the fourth store you've been in,** searching for the glitter-sprinkled blue jeans your seven-year-old has told you are an absolute must for her back-to-school wardrobe. As you push through yet one more clothes rack, you're wondering: Who is the tyrant who decreed these fashion trends for second graders? Or you're shopping for yourself and wishing like crazy that the suit that looks good on you came in the color of the one that doesn't. And again you're asking yourself: Who decides this stuff?

Enter the merchandiser/design director/fashion director. Call him one or all of those titles; the meaning is the same. He's the guy, or gal, for that matter, who puts together the lines of clothing—tops, bottoms, snuggies, sunsuits—we see in the stores. Lines of clothing, that is. Lots of lines per season, lots of seasons per year.

The design director is the guiding light behind most of the clothes we, or our kids, are wearing. While designer brands have their own

Malcolm Drummond has been a design director and
merchandiser for kids' fashions since the 1970s. Every year
he will select and put together four lines of kids' clothes.
And he starts each line a year before you see it in the stores.

well-known and heavily promoted resident geniuses—Donna Karan, Ralph Lauren, for example—the bulk of America's clothing starts in the minds of a design director unknown to the public. And since New York is the fashion capital of America, most of those designers work right here.

Malcolm Drummond has been a design director and merchandiser for kids' fashions since the 1970s. He works now for a New York garment manufacturer of children's clothing. Every year, he will select and put together four lines of kids' clothes—for spring, fall, and two "transition" seasons. And he starts each line a year before you see it in the stores.

Born in the north of England, Drummond was a university student in London during the late 1960s, when that city's Carnaby Street seemed to be the center of world fashion. He interned in the industry and fell under its spell, then set about becoming an expert in the merchandising end of the business, working primarily for retail conglomerates or wholesale suppliers.

Becoming a merchandising expert is not easy. It requires "management skills, fashion sense, technical comprehension, understanding of color, and a flair for design," Drummond says. In short, "a muddle of things."

The work starts with shopping—window-shopping, mostly— in stores, magazines, and, when possible, a trip to Europe.

Why Europe? European kids and teens, this U.S. citizen asserts, are far more individualistic in dress than American kids, who tend to move in packs. Visiting Europe's stores and walking its streets give a merchandiser like Drummond the first outlines of an idea.

What he learns from this preliminary look around is supple-mented by the color trend forecasters (see Color Box story). "They're making predictions ahead of everything," Drummond explains. And supplemented, too, by his own intuition, experience, savvy, and "gut."

The result? A theme for the season a year hence. Actually, Drummond will come up with several themes, enough to cover the four to six merchandise deliveries per season, each of which requires its own fresh look. He'll review the themes with his management and with store buyers, who will add their input. Management might say that the factory can't handle a particular idea, or it might reject a theme that hasn't worked in the past. Store buyers may say they can't sell Malcolm's idea, or they'll gush over another and ask for more along those lines.

Armed with the winnowed field of themes, Drummond will move the merchandising process to the next steps—full-line sketches,

croquis (design sketches from which a pattern can be made) with the full range of colors, and finally samples of everything. At the same time, he'll put together groups of colors for each group of merchandise. In fact, color selection has to be finalized early because the production process for colors is so complex.

Once it's all together, once the colors have been selected and sent off and the samples are approved, it's time for production, some of it in the U.S., much of it overseas. A year after his first look at stores, magazines, and "the street," the line Drummond conceived will finally hit the stores.

"There's a lot of stuff flying at the same time," Drummond says, "and you must keep them flying in formation."

Consider what's in a line. For babies, there are the one- and two-piece sets, dresses, creepers, and rompers—all with permutations. Babies' sleepwear is a separate item altogether, mostly because government regulations about composition and construction are so stringent. For kids, a line will include tops, bottoms, dresses, and two-piece outfits. Again, that means a range of garments for each category—all with different permutations.

Now multiply that by four seasons a year. Spring and fall are the two major seasons, but a holiday season line turns up the glitz for partygoing and marks a fall-into-spring transition. And the back-to-school line keeps the bright colors of summer and serves as a fall-into-spring transition.

The bottom line on all these lines? So many permutations per garment, so many garments per line, so many lines per season, so many seasons per year. It's up to Malcolm Drummond and others like him to keep it coming, keep it fresh and new, gain the edge that catches the eye.

After decades in the business, Drummond both loves it and hates it. On the minus side are how hard the work is, the exhaustion factor, and the difficulty, which crops up more than he'd like, of getting his ideas across. On the plus side are "the creativity, the excitement of discovering new things, and exchanging ideas with people who feel similarly."

Think about it the next time you're shopping for a little romper suit for your favorite toddler.

**The bottom line on all these lines? So many permutations per garment, so many garments per line, so many lines per season, so many seasons per year. It's up to Malcolm Drummond and others like him to keep it coming.**

Some people may grab their car keys to find their way to outdoor adventure. New Yorkers reach for their MetroCards.

# New York Outdoors

**MOST PEOPLE THINK** that when New Yorkers get a yen for the great outdoors, they have to leave town. But as with so many things in our fair city, the obvious doesn't always apply. All kinds of great outdoors are right here in town, waiting at the end of a subway or bus ride. Some people may grab their car keys to find their way to outdoor adventure. New Yorkers reach for their MetroCards.

What's your pleasure? Are you a birder, fisherman, hiker, cyclist? Do you prefer marshland or mountains? Woods or water? You can do it all, have it all, without leaving the city limits. In New York, the great outdoors starts at the doorstep and is limited only by the imagination.

## Only in New York: Race of the High Fliers

**One of the sporting world's** premier competitive events takes place annually in New York City. It draws an estimated 1500 competitors representing some 120 separate teams. It offers $150,000 in prize money, serious change in any league. And it is an event unique to New York, its finish line deep in the heart of Brooklyn.

Yet none of the city's newspapers regularly covers the event. Dignitaries do not show up for the opening bell. And when a born and bred native New Yorker won the event in 2001, the Mayor and City Council did not order a ticker-tape parade down the city's Canyon of Heroes.

To those who follow the sport of pigeon racing, however, the annual Frank Viola Invitational is the Kentucky Derby, the Super Bowl, and the last game of the World Series all rolled into one. It is the highlight of the six-month racing season for homing pigeons. That season starts in April, when birds hatched in preceding years compete over distances from 150 to 500 miles. It enters a second phase in August, when young birds bred that year are liberated for races of from 100 to 400 miles. The Frank Viola Invitational is an October race, the climax of the season.

The eponymous honoree of the Frank Viola Invitational has been racing pigeons since he was a teenager in the 1930s in Borough Park, Brooklyn. Pigeon racing was big back then. Clubs claimed scores of members, even hundreds, and the rooftops of Brooklyn teemed with pigeon lofts. Remember Brando as Terry Malloy in *On the Waterfront?*

Even at its height, however, pigeon racing in the U.S. never gained the popularity it claims in Belgium, France, Spain, or other European countries. There, as Frank Viola reminds a visitor, it is truly a sport of kings. Well, of queens, anyway: Elizabeth II of Britain maintains a royal coop.

Frank Viola is royalty in the American pigeon racing world. Since 1946, when he was mustered out of the Army, he has been breeding

**To those who follow the sport of pigeon racing, the annual Frank Viola Invitational is the Kentucky Derby, the Super Bowl, and the last game of the World Series all rolled into one.**

and caring for pigeons in the loft behind his home on a quiet street in Bensonhurst, Brooklyn. The loft complex is made up of an L-shaped minihouse and another unit atop the nearby garage. Enclosed, ventilated, warm, and sheltered, Frank Viola's loft burbles with the sound of pigeons cooing. Males share egg-sitting duties with breeding females; some pigeons perch while others stand or sit in their nesting cubicles. In the off-season, Frank lets the racing team out in the morning and again in the late afternoon so that they can stretch their wings. Of course, they come home. "That," says Frank, "is all they know."

Why homing pigeons come home remains a mystery that has generated numerous theories and few solid conclusions. The latest thinking attributes an array of internal map-and-compass abilities to the pigeons: an orientation to the sun, perception of the earth's magnetic field, auditory sensitivity to low frequencies, even the ability to smell wind directions. These birds are bred to this. They're a far cry from the ubiquitous New York pigeons that racer owners refer to as street rats.

Breeding homing pigeons, along with everything else about the sport, can be costly. But for Frank Viola and the guys who help out in his loft—Joe "Butch" D'Amato, who comes up from Florida for the Invitational each year; Billy Ferris, who helps clean the coop; Mr. Taiwan, who helps manage Frank's loft—the sport is like no other. It's a passion that, like all passions, defies explanation.

"It's a very good sport," Viola says. "Very interesting. It keeps us out of trouble, too. Like with women: Since you can't do two things at once, racing pigeons keeps you out of trouble."

Which may be why Viola's wife likes the sport, too. "I always know where to find you, Frank," says Kathleen Viola.

Of course, the competitive action is a big part of what pigeon fanciers love. It starts the night before a race, when owners bring their birds to their club—in Viola's case, the Viola Club not far from his house. At the clubhouse, each bird is fitted with a countermark, a specially numbered or coded band on the leg. At the same time, each owner's boxed clock is set, synchronized to the club clock, then sealed. The birds are crated in screened crates, and the crates are also sealed. While club members await the truck that is picking up racers from six

**"It's a very good sport," Viola says. "Very interesting. It keeps us out of trouble, too. Like with women: Since you can't do two things at once, racing pigeons keeps you out of trouble."**

**Homing pigeons average speeds of 45 to 50 miles per hour, depending on wind conditions, and can reach speeds of 60 to 70 miles per hour with a good tailwind.**

or seven other clubs around the area, they may post a bet on their chosen "board bird," the only gambling in which owners indulge.

With all the pigeons loaded, the truck drives through the night to the release point in Pennsylvania, New Jersey, or, for the Viola Invitational, in Ohio. The birds for a particular race must all be liberated at once. Afterward, the liberator phones in the time of release and describes the weather conditions. And for the birds' owners, the wait begins. And continues.

Homing pigeons average speeds of 45 to 50 miles per hour, depending on wind conditions, and can reach speeds of 60 to 70 miles per hour with a good tailwind. Distances are measured from the release point to each loft, and the bird's speed is measured in yards per minute. Race distances range from 100 miles to 250 to the Invitational's 500 to 600. So after the phone call giving the release details, there will be nothing to see for quite a while. Figure about a mile a minute, though, and given the distance to be flown, the breeders have a good idea of when to start scanning the skies. That's when the adrenaline takes over.

Catching sight of your homer wheeling overhead, then heading into the loft, is an unparalleled thrill, say those who know the feeling. But the adrenaline keeps pumping till the bird is in his own loft and counted home.

When Frank Viola's pigeon won the Frank Viola Invitational in 2001, the bird left Cadiz, Ohio at 8:30 a.m. in a northwest wind and clocked in at 2:11 that afternoon. At first, Joe D'Amato thought the arriving avian was just a street rat. But Frank, who lost an eye to an accident during his career as a construction worker, knew the pigeon, now called The Champ, was his own. After the race, Viola was offered $20,000 for The Champ. He turned it down.

There's more to this than money, more even than action. Joe D'Amato explains it this way: "I get an egg and raise a baby chick. If he wins a race, I feel like I just put a kid through college." Viola says he can recognize each of the 250 pigeons in his loft (about 125 of them racers). "It's just like with women," he says, continuing his theme. "Each one is different. And I know each one of them."

# The Staten Island Greenbelt: Country in the City

**On a cool morning in early April,** Patricia O'Malley catches sight of her first Spring Beauties of the season. The delicate, pink-veined white wildflowers, just peeking up out of the leaf litter, are on the side of a path leading away from a pond where O'Malley has been observing a lineup of turtles sunning themselves on a log. At the sound of geese honking overhead, she trains her field glasses on a pair of them as they dive and swerve in the air currents above the pond, then disappear over the forest canopy. After a walk of another three quarters of a mile or so, up a hill, over the top, then down, O'Malley comes to a swamp where brilliantly green fresh shoots of skunk cabbage stand out sharply against the brown mud and pale grasses of the bog.

O'Malley is out for a day's hike in the countryside. But she just hopped the ferry from Manhattan to Staten Island to get here. She is in a place called, appropriately, High Rock Park, designated a national environmental landmark. It is part of the Staten Island Greenbelt, some 2800 acres of public and private land—woods, hills, tidal marshlands, freshwater wetlands, ponds, lakes and creeks that straddle this borough of New York City.

In a near miracle of preservation, much of the Greenbelt remains relatively unchanged since the time of the Revolution. Within its verdant reaches are healthy habitats for native plants, birds, and wildlife— dry zones that support ancient oaks, tulip trees, beech, and hickory, and wetter zones where red maples, white swamp oak, and willow trees grow. The island climate also enables such "southern" species as

persimmon and sour gum to flourish. In the meadows and wetlands are cottontails as high as an elephant's eye, and the largest skunk cabbage ever seen in this area. The area is alive with creatures of the wild. Herons and other waterfowl swoop around the lakes. Turtles bask. Bunnies, chipmunks, and—maybe—a white-tailed deer or two dart about in the woods. Bumblebees hover over wildflowers.

Usually, O'Malley comes here with a group from the Urban Trail Club or the New York Shorewalkers or the Appalachian Mountain Club. She belongs to them all; in fact, she belongs to more. A retired nurse, she spends most weekends going on or leading hikes to unlikely countrified places within the city.

The clubs to which O'Malley belongs represent just some of the hiking organizations that regularly schedule walks, excursions, and treks in and around New York. Their schedules could keep anyone busy every weekend of the year, all year round, without ever leaving the boundaries of the metropolis. You can explore Central Park's waterways, for example, on a six-mile walk that takes you to pond, lake, and waterfall. Or spend a day observing sea and birds in Jamaica Bay Wildlife Refuge, part of the Gateway National Recreation Area, the nation's first urban national park.

But for long stretches of truly wild woods, it's the half-hour ferry ride—at no charge—to Staten Island. The Greenbelt contains more than 30 miles of trails. The trails are maintained by the City of New York/Parks and Recreation Department, by the nonprofit Greenbelt Conservancy that promotes and preserves the Greenbelt, and by volunteers from the Urban Trail Club, the Boy Scouts, and community groups around Staten Island.

O'Malley first joined a hiking organization—the local chapter of the venerable Appalachian Mountain Club—so that her city-reared son would have a way to get into the woods. Then one day she saw a notice about an ecology outing. The word "ecology" seemed freshly minted back then, and O'Malley, by her own admission, "didn't know a geranium from a Spring Beauty."

The outing proved something of a turning point, however; the people who gathered for it eventually formed the nucleus of what became the Urban Trail Club, and O'Malley became one of its founding members. Since then, she has become a passionate amateur botanist and close acquaintance of the city's walking trails.

Slim and agile as a girl, O'Malley sets a good pace on her outings. She wears a trademark wide-brimmed black hat and carries a well-worn blue knapsack. She has hiked in many places on earth—all over Europe, the island of Crete, the western United States, and Canada. But it's a lot less hassle to grab the pack, lock the door of the apartment, and head for the ferry to Staten Island to search for something wonderful, perhaps a great blue heron, in the city's own wilderness.

**O'Malley sets a good pace on her outings. She wears a trademark wide-brimmed black hat and carries a well-worn blue knapsack. She has hiked in many places on earth, but it's a lot less hassle to grab the pack, lock the door of the apartment, and head for the ferry to Staten Island.**

# The First Urban Audubon Center in the United States . . .

### . . . Is in Prospect Park in Brooklyn.

That makes perfect sense to Peter Dorosh and the other 100-plus members of the Brooklyn Bird Club, which Dorosh heads. And it makes perfect sense to Prospect Park partisans, who will tell you that what landscape geniuses Frederick Law Olmsted and Calvert Vaux practiced in Manhattan's Central Park, they perfected in Prospect Park.

The new urban Audubon Center, opened in April 2002, is housed in a picturesque 1905 Beaux Arts boathouse modeled after a 16th-century library in Venice. Badly deteriorated and scheduled for demolition in the mid-1960s, the boathouse was saved when a bunch of determined Brooklynites, including the poet Marianne Moore, organized to rescue it. It's now a nature education center for citified types. There are two floors of exhibits including hanging mobiles that teach bird identification, helpful for New Yorkers most familiar with sparrows and street pigeons.

The restoration of the boathouse coincided with restoration of the artificial lake it once served and the surrounding woodland. And the millions of birds fighting air turbulence and weather on their long flight to or from the tropical regions of the equator are glad of it. To them, the park appears as "one little green spot in a desert of concrete," in Peter Dorosh's description.

Coming north in the spring to establish breeding territory, warblers and other migrants catch sight of this patch of green foliage and blue water and descend for a rest. They refuel on insects or seedlings, rest their wings, and take flight again, heading north along one of the Atlantic flyway's great highways, the Hudson River. In autumn, passerines and raptors descend; in late fall, waterfowl and winter

**The restoration of the boathouse coincided with restoration of the artificial lake it once served and the surrounding woodland. And the millions of birds fighting air turbulence and weather on their long flight to or from the tropical regions of the equator are glad of it.**

species begin to arrive. And of course, with each change of season, the park becomes a stopping-off point on the return journey as birds head back home.

What makes Prospect Park so special, says Dorosh, is that so many species are funneled into this one confined spot. A birder might see, for example, 20 species of warblers, a selection unlikely in the countryside, where the birds are more spread out. This makes Brooklyn an incredible opportunity for birders.

And the birders know it. During the first week of May, you can see groups of them gathering at major park entrances soon after first light. They'll hike into the deepest recesses of the park, train their binoculars overhead, then wait. Bird-watching takes patience.

But once the sun has risen and warmed the air so that insects are lured from their burrows, patience is rewarded. Here come the warblers, most colorful of this region's songbirds. Of the 36 species of warbler found in the Northeast, all may pass through Prospect Park in early May. Wood warblers love the oak trees, Dorosh says. "They wait for the trees to start showing foliage, and then they come to feed on the tassels or on the insects hiding among the tassel seeds or on the surrounding young oak leaves and buds."

New York City birders, like birders everywhere, are an impassioned community. The new Audubon Center will, it is hoped, create even more of them by attracting more birds to the restored habitat. Already some 50 breeding species make their home in the park and an average of 197 other species pass through it in a year. But for birders, more birds is always a good thing.

**But the real New York City sport? Hands down, it's handball—a spare, simple, accessible, four-season sport you can play indoors and out, in sunshine or in clouds.**

**Everybody knows that New York is a great sports town.** There are legendary baseball teams, two football teams, basketball, hockey, and track at Madison Square Garden, the U.S. Tennis Open in Queens.

But the real New York City sport? The quintessential urban game? Hands down, it's handball—a spare, simple, accessible, four-season sport you can play indoors and out, in sunshine or in clouds. Tyrone Snell, president of Our Own Handball Association, newest of the city's handball organizations, says that the heart of the game's appeal is its simplicity. "All you need," Snell says, "is a ball and a wall." And there are plenty of those in New York.

But handball is not only the province of casual players, kids

# They Live for Handball

hanging out for an hour or two batting a ball around. For some, it is a passion, one of the driving forces in their lives.

Take Snell, for example. He started playing handball in junior high school, and except for a brief flirtation with basketball, it has been the sport of his life. So much so that he admits his day job—actually it's a night job, as a tax examiner—mostly subsidizes his involvement with the sport, even as it keeps him from playing as much as he would like.

The passion is widely shared. "People play all day," Snell says, "then go to inside courts to play at night." They play all year round. In the

**All kinds of people play. Snell says he sees a lot of cops playing the game after a tour of duty, a lot of doctors coming around after a hard day in the hospital. "It keeps you sane," he says. "You slam away your anger and frustration."**

winter they head to indoor courts or they shovel the snow off outdoor courts. All kinds of people play. Snell says he sees a lot of cops playing the game after a tour of duty, a lot of doctors coming around after a hard day in the hospital. "It keeps you sane," he says. "You slam away your anger and frustration."

Almost every public park of any size in New York City has a handball court, and if you drop by any of them, you're likely to find someone playing the game. Stop in at Hoover Park in Queens, or Van Cortlandt Park in the Bronx, or West 4th Street in the heart of Manhattan's Greenwich Village. To the handball fan, the crowds of men playing basketball in the courts just beyond the fence sound like a thundering herd of oafish elephants. Basketball suddenly seems a clumsy contest of rough pushing and pounding leaps. By contrast, the four people playing handball doubles exude a purity and intensity that seem downright elegant. The small blue ball whizzes through the air, hits the wall cleanly, angles off it with the precision of a perfect pool shot. Where basketball players collide, shove, and nudge, handballers focus like lasers on the ball, the wall, the placement of the shot. There's something immaculate about it.

Of course, immaculateness is in the eye of the beholder. That doubles match is on the court typically reserved for "the money game." Not all those guys playing handball hour after hour are there because they want to get some exercise. In New York, where people can find a way to turn almost anything into a buck, some people actually make a living— or supplement one, anyway, by playing handball.

In the early 1970s, when fervent handballer Fred Lynch was a young man out of work, he played for $5 a game and knew that if he didn't win a few, he didn't eat that day. It made him a good player. Games go much higher now, and the park pros rarely lose. So if you do wander onto a court, and some fresh-faced player happens to challenge you to a game, check your wallet before you play.

The city once tried to shut down the courts at Sixth Avenue and West 4th Street, Snell recalls, intending to create a garden on this busy corner of Greenwich Village. But the handballers won out over the horticulturists. "This place is a landmark," says Tyrone Snell.

# New York on the Move

**N**EW YORK NEVER STOPS MOVING. Subways and buses roll up and down city streets, cops patrol their beats, taxis cruise. Even such seemingly stationary constructions as bridges move. Some people wonder if all this motion really gets anywhere. The New Yorker's answer is that it doesn't have to; if you're in New York, you're already there.

## Bicycle Cop— He Keeps Central Park Safe

**Believe it or not,** there are some 1300 bicycle-mounted police officers pedaling around New York. Every precinct has a complement of bicycle cops, but police officer Frank Irizarry figures he has the best assignment of any of them.

Irizarry's precinct is Central Park. The beat he patrols is the park's southern end, 59th Street to 72nd Street, from Fifth Avenue to Central Park West.

Irizarry's mountain bike is perfect for patrolling the park. It can go anywhere, on the drives and transverses, the paved walkways, even the bridle paths and soft-surface trails. And if the need arose, Irizarry could take it where there are no paths, making the bike a far more versatile vehicle than the car or three-wheel scooter he uses for patrols in bad weather.

Irizarry, like all the bicycle cops, has undergone rigorous training in all aspects of riding and maintaining a bike, cycling physiology, and such special techniques as using the bike defensively. (This last, intriguing idea he refuses to discuss, not wanting to give any perps a hint on circumventing bike weapons.) As a crime-stopper, the bike has a unique advantage: Lawbreakers or rules violators can't hear it approaching. "I'm stealthy and I'm swift," says Irizarry. Besides, "people just don't expect a cop on a bike."

What is he patrolling for? In the safest precinct in the city and, Irizarry believes, "the safest park in the world," he confronts mostly quality-of-life issues—larcenies usually of unattended property, failure to possess a permit, and the like. Homicides are "nonexistent," he says. Robberies are rare. So is drunkenness, although public drinking, which is illegal, does take place. Even without rowdiness, however, "a lot of people seem to want to use Central Park as their personal entertainment venue," Irizarry says. On a summer weekend, when as many as 200,000 people fill the place, that can cause problems.

To combat whatever he may come up against, Irizarry is equipped with everything he would carry if he were on foot or in an automobile: a firearm and extra rounds, a portable radio, Mace, and his baton—in his case, a collapsible version. In his NYPD bike bag, he carries extra flashlights, binoculars to check out those quality-of-life crimes, and first aid. The first aid is there to handle the numerous scrapes and scratches suffered by in-line skaters, skateboarders, and other cyclists.

On his rounds, he will check permits, ask people to leash their dogs, order a group of guys to take the six-pack and leave the park, please. He reminds people not to leave property unattended—in fact, doing so is grounds for a summons. He answers questions and gives directions—Irizarry must know every tree, flower, and rock in his patrol area.

Still, it's not necessarily an easy beat, and it can be hectic. On a summer weekend, with someone illegally playing bongo drums (you need a permit for that), five kids lost at once, and the temperature hovering at 96 degrees, a cop on a bike really earns his pay.

**Irizarry is equipped with everything he would carry if he were on foot or in an automobile: a firearm and extra rounds, a portable radio, Mace, and his baton—in his case, a collapsible version.**

Winter is a lovely, slow beat for Central Park cops, a time when Irizarry can pay some attention to the beauties of the place while he pedals. He wears a Polartec shirt and a Gore-Tex ski jacket-cum-vest modified to NYPD specifications. In summer, he's in shorts. Winter or summer, he sports a bicycle helmet and a bulletproof vest, the latter standard issue for cops on the street.

And winter or summer, Frank Irizarry loves his job. He loves the park and loves the bicycle. "It's freedom," he says. "It's fun. And it's people-friendly."

That it is. Tag along with Frank Irizarry and you will feel yourself in the presence of a celebrity. Foreign tourists in particular ask if he will pose for a photo with them. Frank throws an arm around these strangers' shoulders and smiles broadly for the camera. All over the world, in living rooms and offices, Frank Irizarry's face must stare out at people from home videos and snapshots.

At night, he loves to see tourists "testing the perimeters" of the park, as he puts it. In thrall to old movies that made Central Park synonymous with danger, wary of the park at night, but clearly lured by its beauty, they'll hover just at the edge of the greenery, uncertain, tempted. Frank Irizarry stands like a host and waves them forward.

"Come on in," he seems to be saying, as if inviting strangers into his home.

## ■ Where Cabdrivers Polish Their Image

**Who would've thought** that New York City cabdrivers care about their image?

Well, they do.

Or at least the Taxi and Limousine Commission, which regulates taxis and other vehicles for hire, cares. And to make sure that image is up to par, the commission sends would-be drivers to a four-hour continuing-education class before giving them a permanent license to operate a medallion cab.

"What do you think is the riding public's image of cabdrivers?"

Andrew Vollo, who himself drove a cab in New York for 15 years, asks the question of 14 drivers who hold probationary licenses and have been on the job less than a year. That brief experience, however,

appears to have been sufficient to cloak the 14 in the brittle carapace of cynicism that is routinely associated with the New York cabbie.

The question raises eyebrows, curls lips, and stuns most into a stony silence. "They think we're reckless," one of the new drivers finally ventures in response. "They think we're trying to cheat them," offers another. "They complain we don't speak English," says a third.

It is a Friday evening in the classroom at LaGuardia Community College in Queens, hour one of the four-hour course. The applicants here have already obtained a New York State chauffeur's license, been drug tested and declared clean, been medically examined and declared fit. He or she has proven proficiency in the English language, has instruction in defensive driving, and, though it might not always seem that way, has passed an 80-hour course in New York's urban geography, map-reading skills, traffic regulations, and the rules of the TLC.

Their probationary hack license is good for one year. Before that year is up, however, and the permanent license granted, a probationary driver must attend the course being offered tonight.

"They think we're reckless," one of the new drivers finally ventures in response. "They think we're trying to cheat them," offers another. "They complain we don't speak English," says a third.

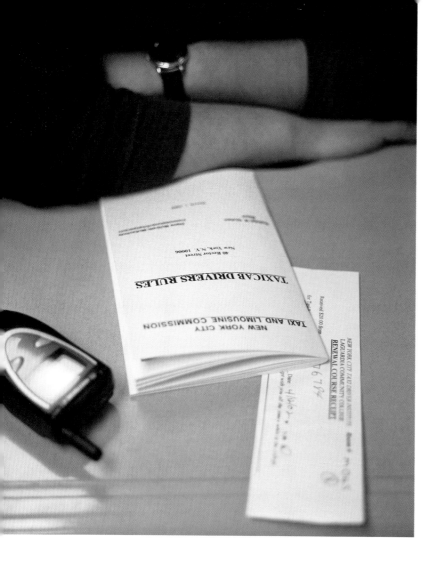

Vollo's students, possibly despite themselves, are intrigued by the issue of their image, although they approach it warily. There's a chip-on-the-shoulder undertone resonating through their disdainful view of how the public views them—a case of launching an offense before you have to put up a defense. In fact, one of the students admits, "only about 30 percent of riders, if that," give him a hard time. The rest, he sounds almost relieved to report, are perfectly pleasant.

It's an opening for Vollo to launch the be-pleasant-proactively part of the course, and he moves right into the opening.

On this particular night, the class is made up entirely of non-native speakers. Most of the group is from the Indian subcontinent, with one Eastern European, one French-accented Haitian, and a Southeast Asian or two. This is by no means unusual, says Barbara Schechter, the TLC deputy commissioner who devised the curriculum for the course. While the TLC does not break out the ranks of drivers by national origin, the clear majority are immigrants, says Schechter, "and that has long been the case." The nationalities change with the immigrant flow into the city as a whole.

Why do immigrants flock to this job that is notoriously nerve-racking, hard on the back, and wearing on the spirit? "It's an entry-level way to get in almost immediately on the American dream," Schechter says. "It's a ladder. At the top of the ladder is owning your own medallion, or a fleet of them. And there are 12,187 medallions out there."

New Yorkers tend to take in stride the changing face, literally, of the city's cabbies, as if each new wave of immigrant driver were just a new accent to get used to, a new kind of music to listen to on the taxi's

**The curriculum for the four-hour course was based on feedback from riders—"consumers," Schechter calls them. "We wanted to make drivers responsive to the consumers they drive," she says, "so we took samplings of both complaints and compliments to show them how to behave, and how not to behave."**

radio. Cranking one's body uncomfortably into the back seat of a yellow New York taxi, hauling briefcase and packages in after you, then looking up to see an elegantly turbaned Sikh at the wheel, or to see a name with no apparent vowels on the photo license, just adds color to the New York mosaic. Besides, maybe your own immigrant father or grandfather drove a cab.

The curriculum for the four-hour course was based on feedback from riders—"consumers," Schechter calls them. "We wanted to make drivers responsive to the consumers they drive," she says, "so we took samplings of both complaints and compliments to show them how to behave, and how not to behave." Biggest complaints: rudeness, refusal of service, and lack of knowledge about where something was located.

The course focuses first on the rules and regulations of operating a taxi, then on driver-passenger relations, using lots of student participation and role-playing, then on transporting passengers with disabilities. Drivers are also taught what the law requires of them, whether it's stowing a wheelchair or making room for a service animal.

By the end of the four hours, Vollo's students have softened. His persistent reminder that "the better you customize a ride, the better the tip" has begun to make sense. His ideas about setting the right tone—"The most important part of a trip is the first minute," he insists—and about engaging the rider in making the trip pleasant have begun to wear away the sullen distrust that many probationary drivers have spent a year acquiring, as if it were part of the standard cabbie uniform. Maybe he's right, they have begun to think. Maybe this is a business I can build better if I do these things.

"For those who want to make it work," says Barbara Schechter, "the course provides tools they can take advantage of. And the ones who get out there and use the tools invariably get positive reinforcement, so they keep it up."

Vollo even offers a tip for back pain—a medical recommendation that a driver get out of the cab, move, and stretch after every fare. The students whistle collectively. After every fare? Well, Vollo agrees, a few times a day, in any event.

He makes no suggestions for dealing with the traffic, however.

## Where Does All That Subway Garbage Go?

**Have you ever stood in a subway station late at night,** weary, just wanting to go home? You hear a sound from up the tunnel and inch toward the edge of the platform. A train at last! You will see your own living room tonight after all.

Then you read the NOT IN SERVICE sign on the front of the train. It whizzes by you, literally leaving you in the dust.

This train is not for you. It's for garbage. It's the refuse train on its nightly run, heading from the top of Manhattan to eastern Queens and back again, collecting trash along the way.

This is what happens to all that subway station trash—the newspapers, candy wrappers, coffee cups, tissues, and other detritus that subway riders drop in the big black solar cans, as they are called, on the subway platforms. Six times a day—twice per shift on three shifts per day—station cleaners empty the filled bags out of the solar cans and put in new ones. They deposit the bulging bags in rolling canisters stored in a locked refuse room or, in small stations, in a locked metal cabinet. The refuse train collects the trash by night and deposits it at the yard in the morning, when trucks arrive to haul it to a landfill.

There are seven refuse trains in all. They operate out of four yards,

one each in Manhattan, the Bronx, Brooklyn, and Queens. Refuse trains follow their own special routes, using the tracks of various lines to cover their particular territory. The refuse train on the A track switches to F tracks to go down Manhattan and into Brooklyn, rides north and east through Queens, then returns via A tracks again to the yard at 207th Street. No passenger train does that.

Crew members arrive at the Manhattan yard, at 207th Street, to start their shift at 8 p.m. The train pulls up, and the first job is to load empty canisters aboard the flatbed freight cars that actually haul the trash. The guys let down the sides of the flats, then slide the empty canisters aboard.

**This train is not for you. It's for garbage. It's the refuse train on its nightly run, heading from the top of Manhattan to eastern Queens and back again, collecting trash along the way.**

It's time to board. The crew might spread out in the retired passenger cars that serve to pull or push the train, but for the most part, these cars have been retired because they're "scrap," says Jose Riano, who oversees this refuse train. So instead, the crew gathers in a special car at the back of the train, complete with benches, tables, and lockers.

Varoom. The train stumbles forward, picks up speed, and rumbles downtown on the A-train's track, disappointing all those passengers waiting for trains in the stations.

Between 81st and 72nd streets, the train is switched onto a side track while other trains hurtle past. At its first stop at 53rd and Seventh, the crew hops out. Two crew members lower the sides of the flats. The key operator opens the refuse room. "Two!" he calls out. The men haul two canisters off the flats and exchange them for the filled cans from the refuse room. Supervisor Riano oversees the operation, which takes minutes. "Most stops take a minute or two," he says, "but a stop like Parsons/Archer way out in Queens has so much stuff it can take 45 minutes." The flats are locked, the crew hops aboard, and the refuse train continues its nightly run.

## Retractile Bridges: Only Four Left, And New York's Got the Only Two That Work

**Retractiles, which date back to medieval times, are movable bridges that withdraw to shore horizontally.**

**New York is unique in many ways.** But one of its more obscure, and endearing, unique features is its maintenance of an ancient bridge type called a retractile. Only four remain in the United States, and of those, the two that work are in our fair city.

Retractiles, which date back to medieval times, are movable bridges that withdraw to shore horizontally. Because they gobble up precious waterfront when clinging to a shoreline, they are an inefficient use of land, and so out of favor in these crowded times. On the other hand, retractiles need relatively modest equipment and use relatively little power. And they are ideal for use over narrow waterways.

Like the narrow Gowanus Canal in the borough of Brooklyn, home to the oldest known extant retractile in the United States. The bridge, built in 1889, was originally powered by steam and is now powered by electricity. But it is still operated by hand, as it always has been. Specifically by the hand of Leonard Thomas, the bridge operator in charge of three Gowanus bridges: the bascule bridges at 3rd Street and Union Street, and the unique retractile at Carroll Street.

To operate his bridges, Thomas must step lively. Maritime law requires that a bridge must open for any marine purpose, although two-hour notice is mandated. And there is plenty of maritime traffic entering the Gowanus Canal from the Gowanus Bay. (Both named for the Indian chief who originally sold off the land). To clear the canal for the traffic, Thomas, who is stationed at the Union Street bridge, hops in his car to open the 3rd Street Bridge first, then close the bridge there. Then he drives to Carroll Street to open and close the bridge there, then back to Union Street. When the traffic returns down the canal to the Bay, it must back out, and Thomas opens and closes his three bridges in reverse order: Union Street, Carroll Street, 3rd Street.

If you're ever driving on Carroll Street, a one-way thoroughfare heading east, and the pintle gates at either end of the bridge are

**Thomas is inside the control room, getting ready to open his bridge. He sounds a horn, then he levers the controls, and the bridge begins to move.**

closed, you'll know that Thomas is inside the control room, getting ready to open his bridge. He sounds a horn, then he levers the controls, and the bridge begins to move.

Inside the control room is the mechanism's sizable winch. The winch drum is grooved for two wire ropes, each a mere inch in diameter. Both ropes are attached to the movable structure of the bridge, one for opening, the other for closing. In a sense, the mechanism works on a push-pull basis. When Thomas opens the bridge, a wire rope pulls the movable structure horizontally to lie along the west side of the canal; in closing, the mechanism pushes it back.

There has been a bridge over this point on the Gowanus Canal since it was constructed in the 1860s, to serve fast-growing Brooklyn, then a separate city from New York. In due course, small industries sprung up along the two-mile canal, along with residential communities for the industry workers. Inevitably for the day, pollutants from the commercial and human population turned the waterway noxious and fetid, and by the midpoint of the next century, both industry and the neighborhood were in decline. Traffic along the canal abated, but never stopped entirely.

Today, the neighborhood is on the upswing, once again combining residences and commercial activity. The community sees the canal as the inspiration for its revitalization, and the retractile bridge at Carroll Street as a city treasure.

And when the bridge operator is not opening or closing it, he is probably cooking chicken. Lenny Thomas is the author of *Cooking with the Chicken Man*, in which he offers one hundred all-chicken-all-the-time recipes plus stories to go with them. Thomas has been opening bridges since 1975, and he has been cooking chicken for even longer. He does both well.

## Riding the NYC Greenway, What There Is of It

One day, or so the powers that be tell us, there will be 350 miles of greenway in New York.

**Three cyclists emerge from a dark woods** and top the rise on the bridge over Francis Lewis Boulevard in Queens, where they halt for water and a look at a map. Below them, traffic streams thunderously in both directions. Around them, birds are chirping noisily, almost noisily enough to drown out the traffic sounds. The cyclists are on a portion of the 22-mile Queens Greenway that pretty much circles the borough through parks and cemeteries and city streets. Except for the streets, which the bikes perforce share with auto traffic, the mostly paved greenway path is reserved for nonmotorized traffic—bicycles, skates, scooters, maybe a baby carriage or wheelchair.

One day, or so the powers that be tell us, there will be 350 miles of greenway in New York. The city will be crisscrossed by a network of transportation and recreation paths that follow both natural and man-made lines—abandoned railroad rights-of-way, parklands, waterfront esplanades, bridges,

ferry crossings, and side roads along highways. Eighty percent of the system will be traffic-free, buffered in some way from motorized traffic. The different greenways will be linked within and across boroughs, so that you will be able to ride safely and happily from, say, Coney Island at the bottom of Brooklyn to Fort Totten at the top of Queens, along the way experiencing waterfront and woods, urban architecture and ethnic neighborhoods.

In addition, the city greenway system will be connected to two long-distance trails, the Hudson River Greenway connecting the city to Albany and Montreal, and the East Coast Greenway, stretching from Maine to Florida.

**The different greenways will be linked within and across boroughs, so that you will be able to ride safely and happily from, say, Coney Island at the bottom of Brooklyn to Fort Totten at the top of Queens.**

The idea for a greenway system goes back as far as Frederick Law Olmsted, the genius designer of parks. Olmsted envisaged Brooklyn's Eastern and Ocean parkways as wide boulevards stretching east deep into Queens and south to the ocean, uniting parks and people, bikes and beaches, the city and the country and the sea. In the 1930s, master builder Robert Moses, notorious for wanting to put a highway through everything, also expanded pedestrian walkways in the parks and built bicycle paths along many roads. Later, citizen activists, like those of the Neighborhood Open Space Coalition, took a passionate leading role in supporting the creation of greenways. Finally in 1991, Congress made funds available for greenways nationwide. In 1993, New York City published a Greenway Plan covering the five boroughs.

Almost by definition, implementation of the plan can only move slowly, mile by difficult mile, "little pieces at a time," says Jack Schmidt, director of the transportation division at the City Planning Commission. But then, nobody is waiting around for the completion of the entire Greenway Plan. For roller skaters, walkers, cyclists, and anyone who wants to go on traffic-free strolls, the greenways, even in their current patchwork state, are a godsend.

The cyclists emerging from the woods are members of the Five Borough Bicycle Club, which runs day trips in and around the city every weekend of the year. A single Saturday or Sunday trip of the 5BBC, as it's called, will attract anywhere from five to 40 trippers—the lower number for the Frostbite rides in winter, a good 35 to 40 for the Beach Bum rides in summer.

A typical Beach Bum ride might start at Brooklyn's Prospect Park and end at Neponsit Beach in Rockaway, Queens, just next to the Gateway National Recreation Area. On a hot day, a leisurely pace is called for, and it might take the group two hours, including snack stops, to get to Neponsit. Leaving the park, the cyclists will follow side streets to Sheepshead Bay, where they will turn onto the designated greenway along the Shore Parkway, and eventually make their way to the beautiful Rockaway Gateway Greenway and the beach. After a couple of hours of sun and surf, they'll cycle back the way they came, possibly detouring to Brooklyn College to see the parrots that have nested on the stadium lights of the football field.

The parrots, it is said, escaped from cargo at JFK Airport in 1997 or so and were not expected to live through the winter. They easily confuted that expectation, however, and are thriving in Brooklyn. And while they have become a nuisance to the neighborhood around the stadium, they are beautiful to look at—like brilliant green pigeons. Another odd and intriguing city sight to bike to.

# Those Traffic Signs— New York's Required Reading

**To keep New Yorkers on the move safely**—and legally—the city maintains, it will probably come as no surprise, the largest sign manufacturing operation in the country. New York produces, from scratch, some 70,000 signs per year for the streets of the five boroughs. And all the signs are manufactured in the same place, at the Signs and Markings department of the city's Department of Transportation, creators of New York's required reading.

Just how many of those signs are there? Don't bother to guess; the number changes all the time. The signs cover the gamut of mobility needs. There are highway signs that tell you where you're going, and that you've arrived. There are "advance signs," warning you of an overpass, school crossing, or speed bump up ahead. If you need further help, the signs are color-coded. Advisory signs (SLOW DOWN, CHILDREN CROSSING) have black type on a yellow background. Regulatory signs (NO LEFT TURN) have black type on white. Parking meter signs are green and white; parking regulations are red on white, and parking prohibitions are white on red.

New York produces, from scratch, some 70,000 signs per year for the streets of the five boroughs.

There are blue-and-white signs for hospitals and orange-and-black signs for warnings. There are the nighttime parking regulation signs with white stars on a black expanse of sky and the red broom icon of the Sanitation Department, early harbingers of a trend toward universal symbols.

There are, says David Leschke, the director of the Maspeth Central Shop, the tiny riders attached to signs mandating parking for authorized vehicles only; the riders tell you who's authorized. There are the huge signs— 12 feet by eight feet—that announce that NEW YORK CITY WELCOMES NELSON MANDELA! Or NEW YORK CITY WELCOMES THE GRAMMY AWARDS! There is the 35 foot by 12 foot New York City Marathon sign that hangs on the Queensboro Bridge and the special blue line on the roadway from the Staten Island side of the Verrazano-Narrows Bridge through every borough to the finish line in Central Park.

**And there are the 1200-plus signs delivered in a single month following the events of September 11, 2001, when entire routes had to be changed and new passageways created to keep the city open and alive.**

And there are the 1200-plus signs the Maspeth shop delivered in a single month following the events of September 11, 2001, when entire routes had to be changed and new passageways created to keep the city open and alive.

At the Maspeth shop, the multi-acre stockroom sits behind high wire fencing. The signs are neatly stacked in rows, each with its own reference number. In a corner of the depot is the mammoth line-painting truck, called the Nightliner, with its Rube Goldberg–like pipes and gizmos and tanks. The truck makes it possible to mark the Marathon route in only two nights with temporary latex paint.

Signs are ordered by DOT's design and construction office. "The text determines the size of a sign," says Leschke. For highway signs, speed and height are also factors: A highway sign must be big enough and high enough for a driver to take in when driving at 55 miles an hour and craning to see over the tops of trucks and buses.

Leschke has been at Maspeth since 1978, a time when letters in different sizes were kept in bins and signmakers applied the letters one at a time to each sign. It's a long way from that to the highly mechanized silk-screening that can churn out 5000 small signs a week or to the computer-aided design that lets someone like Lisa Hall, trained at the High School of Art and Design and at Parsons, turn out some 15 two-sided traffic or road signs per day.

How long do signs last? Leschke says they would last to the specifications laid down for their components "in a perfect world—but that's not something we have here." The life span of a highway sign, for example, could be 20 years. But, says Leschke, "pollution, salt, and weather corrode the reflective sheeting, or maybe the sign gets hit by a truck that doesn't clear. So it has to be replaced."

Signs and Markings, let's be clear, merely delivers signs to the boroughs. It installs nothing. "The borough DOT orders, we manufacture, and they install," says Leschke. "Without here," he adds in perfect New Yorkese, "it doesn't happen."

*The medium may be paint or performance, visual, auditory, the Internet, or chalk on a sidewalk.*

# Living the Artist's Life

**NEW YORK IS HOME** to several of the planet's greatest museums, to what is possibly the nation's—even the world's—most important newspaper, to the major television networks and publishing houses. That's the tip of the iceberg.

Beneath the waterline is a world of artistic endeavors tucked away in hidden corners, appealing to a particular niche in the city. The locale may be a whole neighborhood or a single street. The audience may be defined by language or ethnic group, by political inclination, by religion, passion, or outlook. The medium may be paint or performance, visual, auditory, the Internet, or chalk on a sidewalk. The permutations are endless.

And they generate an ongoing cycle. Creative people are drawn to the bubbling ferment of New York's art and media worlds. They come here to make more art and to innovate new media in a ceaseless flow—the ultimate perpetual-motion machine.

## The Art Gallery in the Fish Market

**At Manhattan's Fulton Fish Market,** downtown in one of the city's oldest neighborhoods, the workday starts in the shadowy hours before dawn. Workers materialize out of the dark, making their way to the locked buildings to open the market to the city.

But as soon as the day becomes lighter, light enough to paint by, you might see Naima Rauam hauling her easel through the district's streets. She's usually in place by 6 a.m. or so. When the light moves, she moves with it, down one street or across another. Naima is The Lady Who Paints Fish. And the fish market itself. And the people in it. For a reason even she cannot explain clearly, she is drawn to the bustling, cavernous, open-air center that sells everything from tiny rock shrimp to thousand-pound swordfish.

Naima first encountered the Fulton Fish Market when she was a student at the legendary Art Students League, and she never forgot it. For a while, life carried her down other paths, to a career as a commercial artist, to marriage and a home in Maine. But when her husband died in 1983, Naima came back to New York. And the market.

She set up her easel and started to paint. In time, she got to know the "fish guys" who worked in the market and the neighborhood regulars. She began to build a body of art, dedicated almost entirely to this corner of the city, this unique moment that occurs every morning of every weekday.

When summer ended and the weather turned cold, Rauam asked the fish guys if anyone had any free space. She found some in the back of a smoked-fish wholesaling shop at 146 Beekman Street. There, she could work, and in the afternoons, when the fish business had closed for the day, the proprietors allowed her to show her paintings, turning the space into a kind of gallery. She called it Art in the Afternoon, Fish in the Morning. Her pictures were displayed on the scales used for weighing the fish, on the countertops, and on the cutting and slicing equipment. Guests at the opening of the gallery were treated to wine, cheese, and smoked fish. Rauam had become the unofficial artist-in-residence of the Fulton Fish Market.

What is at the heart of this inspiration? Ask Rauam and she will give you a number of answers. It's the history of the place, the continuity of a market that has been in existence in this spot since 1821. It's the physical setting, a group of ramshackle buildings that unfold

**In the afternoons, when the fish business had closed for the day, the proprietors allowed her to show her paintings ... displayed on the scales used for weighing the fish.**

**It's the work the fish guys do, real, physical, meaningful. A million pounds of fish move through here each night, Rauam says, "and people are constantly hauling it, cutting it, moving it."**

naturally. It's the work the fish guys do, real, physical, meaningful. A million pounds of fish move through here each night, Rauam says, "and people are constantly hauling it, cutting it, moving it." It's the light, intense work lights spotlighting activity in the dark, sleeping city. It's everything: the piles of boxes, the movement, the close-knit community.

One forty-six Beekman has been sold, and Rauam now shows her work at the South Street Seaport Museum. She's painted other settings over the years, of course. She's been enamored of construction sites, bridge cables, and airplanes (she's a licensed pilot), and has painted them all. But the fish market continues to dominate her work. For this New Yorker, it's her artistic home.

**On the corner of 44th Street and Tenth Avenue,** in the middle of Hell's Kitchen, above a parking lot and across the street from a bodega is a glorious painting. It's difficult to say exactly what it is. An arched entry to—something. The arches themselves are beautiful, uplifting, but belong to no particular tradition. The painted tiles of the floor look—Mediterranean? Maybe.

The mural has no title and is not signed. But it is highly visible. It can be seen from boats passing by on the Hudson, trucks and taxis whizzing by Tenth Avenue, and by Hell's Kitchen inhabitants. Its fame has spread; she has heard from people from Turkey, Italy, France, and

## She Brought Raphael to Hell's Kitchen

Yemen who have seen and loved it. It has done what its creator, Edla Cusick, wanted it to do: transport those who see it to another place in their minds.

Not too long ago, the wall—the west wall of the Holy Cross Convent on West 44th Street, was covered with a hodgepodge of ugly graffiti. Cusick, an artist who lives on the street, watched as the nuns in the convent fought a losing battle with the graffiti. It would appear; they would cover it up. A few days later it was back again.

Cusick didn't much care for the graffiti, but she understood the kids who climbed on the cars of the parking lot to paint the wall. She felt the same impulse. A huge wall—55 feet by 58 feet, in this case—is to an artist what a siren song is to a sailor—an irresistible lure. Cusick heard the song. But there was more to it than that.

She didn't want to merely paint the wall; she wanted to paint something that would be a gift to the people who pass through the neighborhood, now a mixed bag of old tenements and high-priced renovations. Elderly Irish alongside young Hispanics, blacks, and Asians.

For Cusick, the heart and soul of the neighborhood expressed itself in the taxi drivers she saw coming to work at a nearby garage each morning, with their thermoses of coffee or tea. Primarily Asian and Arab, they seemed to her the lifeblood of New York, the most recent in a long line of contributors to the city's diversity.

"I wanted to create a big image for them," she recalls, "something peaceful and simple and clean. I wanted each one to feel lightened for a moment and perhaps to think, 'That looks like my country.'"

The challenge was twofold. The artistic challenge was to find a culturally neutral image that would achieve Cusick's goal—and then to execute it, no small task for a painter of canvases who had no idea how to paint a wall. The other challenge was more basic—how to find the money to fund it.

**She envisaged the shape of an arch, but not one that belonged to any particular culture or faith.**

The nuns who owned the wall, and the local community board, approved of the idea, but neither could offer money to help make it a reality. So Cusick went around the neighborhood, buttonholing shopkeepers and merchants for contributions. She wrote letters to foundations and rich people and friends, anyone she could think of who might want to see a beautiful wall in New York City. Finally the money was raised from "very generous donors." Now Cusick could turn to the mural itself.

She had decided that the image should be "an illusion of a place, an opening up of the wall." She envisaged the shape of an arch, but not one that belonged to any particular culture or faith. That meant it couldn't be a Moorish arch that would resonate in a particular way with Muslims, nor a distinctively Christian or Roman arch. It had to speak to both Muslims and Christians—and everybody else, for that matter.

Cusick began to research arches. As the vision came into sharper focus, she saw the arches standing on a floor against a landscape. She began to research those images as well, poring over art books she hadn't opened since she was a student at the Art Students League.

She found the floor she wanted in Raphael's painting of *The*

*School of Athens*, in the Vatican Museums in Rome. The landscape colors—Cusick calls them "corny, hot, crazy" colors—were inspired by the works of Maxfield Parrish. For a long time, the arch itself escaped her, but at last she saw what she wanted in the service entrance of an old apartment building. Art is where you find it.

With all the elements in place in her mind, Cusick created a small painting of the mural she envisioned. Now she needed someone who could translate that small image onto a huge brick wall.

Enter Paul Chan, "the last of the wall painters," Cusick says. Chan once had a thriving specialty creating advertisements riding high up on the sides of New York's buildings. But today, computers have taken over all that. Chan's way of painting a wall—a human being standing on a scaffold painting onto the wall surface—is virtually obsolete. Chan, himself an immigrant who learned his art in his native Hong Kong, today produces shop signs and paints and repaints the huge Mets banner on the grass at Shea Stadium. And he still handles an occasional mural commission.

Standing on a scaffold above the parking lot on Tenth Avenue at 44th Street, he created a grid, then used outdoor enamel paint to create Cusick's mural. He began painting in November 1994 and finished six weeks later, positioning most of the image out of reach of kids armed with spray paint. Cusick made sure to keep extra cans of the floor colors. She figured it was still possible for the graffiti-minded to reach as far up as the Raphael floor portion, and her plan was "to go back out and partially cover each new graffiti mark so I would eventually build up a crazy-quilt look."

It didn't happen. There has only been one rather indifferent graffiti "hit," and Cusick covered it fully. She has heard that graffiti-writers respect perspective. In any event, they left the Raphael-Cusick floor alone.

By now the mural's colors have faded ever so slightly, and Cusick thinks it looks even better this way. If she ever thought the wall would make her rich and famous, she does not seem unhappy that it hasn't. It has done exactly what she wanted it to do. "It took people out of their daily 'whatever' and brought them to this place," she says, to this illusion of some beautiful entrance to some unknown place.

"I have in my pocket the ability to say 'I made this,'" says the artist.

**By now the mural's colors have faded ever so slightly, and Cusick thinks it looks even better this way. If she ever thought the wall would make her rich and famous, she does not seem unhappy that it hasn't.**

# Performance Artists Hidden in Alphabet City

**On the Lower East Side of New York,** behind a steel-gray door that you have to know about to know about, a group of performers are entertaining 20 people on a Friday night. The audience sits no more than 30 feet from any performer at any time. A hilarious video, projected on the wall, sets the tone of no-holds-barred mischief that will be the theme for the evening—late evening.

The proceedings here, scheduled for 10 p.m., don't get under way till around 10:30. It's not what you'd call an early-to-bed crowd. A performer named Zero Boy kicks things off with ironic sketches in sound, and a history of violent weaponry figures prominently. He is followed by William Lee, one of the driving forces behind the group, in the role of Master Kung Fu. With a puppet and two actors, Lee offers biting political satire on timely topics, some of it scripted, some improvised in response to audience questions.

William Lee, a refugee from more traditional performances, is emblematic of the cutting-edge artists centered in the heart of today's neighborhood-in-the-ascendant, the alphabet-soup of avenues at the eastern edge of what has traditionally been called the Lower East Side. Tompkins Square and the streets around it are the unofficial center of the neighborhood. In the apartments above newly chic restaurants and shops, and behind nondescript steel doors that look like they might lead to storage rooms, New York's emergent artists are at work on today's alternative art and alternative lifestyles. They are creating videos and computer-generated happenings. They are writing screenplays, video vignettes, Internet dramas. They are re-thinking art and the arts.

By plan or by fortune, many of these artists create mostly for each other and their friends. They're usually not listed in guides or newspapers, at least not the ones most people read. But if you wander around the

area, latish, you will probably stumble on a happening or two.

For William Lee and his colleagues, the art is performance. Lee conceives, writes, and creates performance projects. Some of his colleagues are actors. One is a magician who turned to sword swallowing. Another worked on the Letterman show, hated it, and now does monologues.

You can also catch William, and others, at open-mike evenings at clubs on Allen or Ludlow streets, in a part of the city that was once a cauldron of immigrant life, not art. The old tenements are still there, but now they house clubs with names like Surf Reality and Collective Unconscious. For a few dollars, anyone can buy eight minutes of stage time and a chance to try anything, to gauge audience response, to refine, to fail utterly. "People do some really crazy things," Lee says, but they often result in good work.

Lee has done stand-up comedy in clubs and on television for years, appearing on the likes of *Late Night with Conan O'Brien*, *Caroline's Comedy Hour*, and *Sesame Street*, as well as on British TV. He has also acted in such dramas as *The Equalizer*. The stand-up, he says "was paying dues," laying the groundwork. What he's doing now—the performing, the writing, the alternative creating—is his true passion.

**Today, the act that Lee takes to fringe performance festivals, street fairs, and parks helps subsidize the writing, and keeps him in front of audiences.**

Today, the act that Lee takes to fringe performance festivals, street fairs, and parks helps subsidize the writing, and keeps him in front of audiences. The writing tends to be political. A project inspired by the idea of Salvador Dali as a magician was emerging as of this writing. Lee wasn't sure what form it would take—"maybe a play, maybe a variety piece, maybe a one-man performance." All he knew for sure was that the piece would include the mating dance of the mackerel, and that he would pull a squid out of his pants and paint a picture of the squid with the ink.

Duck when you see the ink!

## From Graffiti Perps to Corporate Artists

**It's a long way from stealing a can of spray paint** and sneaking into a subway depot to owning a client list that reads like a combination of the Fortune 500 and the guestlist of the Indie Spirit Awards. But that is exactly the journey that a group of Bronx graffiti artists have made.

The group is known as Tats Cru—it's an anagram for something, and besides, they like the way it looks. It was started in 1994 by Bronx natives and dedicated graffiti artists Bio, Nicer, and BG 183, the names they used to sign their once illegitimate art. Today, Tats Cru is a group of 12 "Artists for the New Millennium," as they call themselves. For a

fee, they will spray-paint murals, vehicles, memorial walls, or anything else you want painted. They also design promotional campaigns and Web-site art. They are in the business of "marketing customized aerosol art to businesses," as their own Web site declares.

There was a time, back in the 1970s and early 1980s, when graffiti were the scourge of New York. Upright citizens regarded kids with spray cans much the same way 5th-century Romans looked at Visigoths.

To be sure, a few voices were raised suggesting that graffiti represented a valid form of artistic expression, an outlet for those to whom other outlets were closed. But to most, graffiti were the signature of a city that was in decline. They wanted the "art" out of sight, and they wanted the self-styled graffiti artists out of town or in jail.

But time has brought legitimacy to the outlaw art. Monikers that once raised the ire of cops and building owners—Taki 182, Seen, Dust—are today revered as old masters of an art form that has swept the world.

Founded in 1994 by Bronx natives and dedicated graffiti artists Bio, Nicer, and BG 183, Tats Cru is now a group of 12 "Artists for the New Millennium," as they call themselves. For a fee, they will spray-paint murals, vehicles, memorial walls, or anything else you want painted.

Graffiti art today commands serious attention. And it can command serious sums of money. Graffiti artists have found ways to make a living—not an arrest record—through their art.

Bio remembers being arrested "once or twice" when he was a kid, although there is little evidence in today's solid, middle-aged, business

owner of the one-time mischievous perp. He first became interested in graffiti back when he was fourteen. Older mentors filled him in on "how to get paint and how to sneak into where the subway cars were kept"—the basics. Then it was a matter of learning by doing, exploring techniques to match a flourishing creativity. Graffiti, says Bio, "was a way to be recognized." And for him it was also the only art available.

None of the Tats Cru artists, six full-time and six freelance, has been to art school. BG remembers a paint-by-numbers kit when he was a kid, and he remembers his older sister showing him how to draw. He learned how to use spray paint because it was the material at hand. On a section of the massive mural that adorns the Tats Cru wall at The Point, a complex serving the Hunts Point neighborhood in the Bronx, BG has painted a lavender panel depicting scenes from the countryside of Japan.

It is representational, delicate, almost anachronistic in the midst of the outsized, flamboyant mural. It's a skill he picked up.

There are subtleties to graffiti art. Different effects require different caps, the actual caps on the aerosol cans, according to an artist named Nosm. He is one of a pair of brothers who came to Tats Cru from Germany to pursue their graffiti art. "Skinnies," explains Nosm, provide a cleaner, finer line than fat caps, which tend to overspray and

**Time has brought legitimacy to graffiti art. Names that once resounded like wanted posters in police precincts—Taki 182, Seen, Dust—are today revered as old masters of an art form that has swept the world.**

leave a drip. There are German skinnies and New York skinnies. The German ones are considered to be better.

The Tats Cru supply room is piled high with crates of spray paint of varied type, color, and cap configuration so artists can pull precisely what they need. Nosm has worked on car washes, trailers, and small-business vehicles that serve as moving advertisements. There are odder painting surfaces. Before emigrating to the United States, Nosm painted a tank in Czechoslovakia.

**There are subtleties to graffiti art. Different effects require different caps, the actual caps on the aerosol cans.**

But because the spray paint fumes persist, it is not recommended for houses or apartments. It's an outside kind of art—although no longer an outsider.

Each year, the Cru creates a new giant mural on the wall of The Point—not as a commercial venture but "just to do it." Key to the tradition is to paint the mural as an international collaboration. They gather artists from abroad and start with a sketch. The space they will paint is huge—maybe 20 feet high, Bio estimates, and probably 80 feet long, although he has never measured it. First, they paint over last year's mural. Then each of the artists contributes a section and signs it with his graffiti moniker: Bio, How, Duro3, Sen2, Dawn, Ron, PT.

It feels good to go back to their roots in the early days of open-space graffiti, the artists say. Only this time, they have permission.

# Brooklyn, Home of the Best Egyptian Art

**If you want to see the best in Egyptian art,** get on the subway and go to—Brooklyn.

Brooklyn?

Yes, Brooklyn.

To historians, collectors, and curators who specialize in ancient Egypt, the word Brooklyn isn't so much a place as an adjective. Its meaning? The highest standard of excellence. In these circles, saying something is "Brooklyn quality" is instant jargon for saying its top of the line, the standout in its class.

There are two reasons for this. One is the Egyptian collection in the Brooklyn Museum of Art. The collection contains some 8000 objects—about a tenth of which may be on view at any one time—illustrating every era of ancient Egyptian art and artifact. Other museums may own a greater number of *objects*, but many experts say that Brooklyn's collection houses the highest percentage of *masterpieces*.

Reason two is the museum's Wilbour Library of Egyptology. "Everything you need to know about ancient Egypt is here," says Deirdre Lawrence, the museum's principal librarian and coordinator of research services.

No Egyptian scholar would disagree with her. The Wilbour's 40,000-plus volumes cover the gamut of Egypt's history from the Paleolithic Era to the Islamic Period. The collection is the most comprehensive research library for ancient Egypt in the Western Hemisphere, with second place going to the combined libraries of the Egyptian Museum in Cairo and the Griffith Institute at Oxford University.

In the world of scholarship and museums, Brooklyn's one-two Egyptology punch—the collection and the research facilities that illumine it—are quite simply a knockout.

Charles Edwin Wilbour, for whom the library is named, was an amateur scholar but a passionate and astute Egyptologist, a collector with a fine eye, and an observant note-taker. Voyaging up and down the Nile on his boat, *The Seven Hathors,* he would annotate published texts with his own observations. These marginal corrections and expansions, along with the published records they interpolate, are an important resource of

**Other museums may own a greater number of objects, but many experts say that Brooklyn's collection houses the highest percentage of masterpieces.**

information, particularly about monuments that have since been damaged or destroyed. They are supplemented by the detailed letters Wilbour wrote about his travels. In addition, he was a relentless collector of books, objects, and above all, papyri of very high quality and scholarly importance.

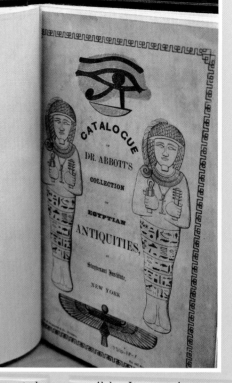

Wilbour died in 1896. His children donated his collection to the Brooklyn Museum and established an endowment in his memory, which made the Library of Egyptology possible. It contains great treasures: 17 Aramaic papyri dating from 449–400 BC, for example, or the extraordinary 18th- and 19th-century travel guides that Wilbour carted around and wrote in, with their fastidious drawings of the ancient monuments of that era. A 1757 volume contains a drawing of the sphinx, made in 1739 or 1740, showing it with smashed nose, thus giving the lie to the commonly repeated canard that Napoleon's troops defaced the great monument. On the contrary: Egyptians themselves appear to have defaced this and many monuments, evidently as a means of protection against dead enemies.

Only five readers per day are granted access to the library, although the museum is open year-round to the public. The library's great value is that so many things are concentrated in one place. It isn't that the Wilbour contains things you can't find elsewhere. The books, periodicals, maps, photographs, and databases that fill its stacks and computers are not unique to Brooklyn. But it's all there in one room—or can all be accessed from this one room. The result is one-stop shopping for scholars.

The interest in ancient Egypt has never abated. Something about that desert land captures the imagination and draws people to learn more about it. Today, new sources of scholarship are coming to the fore from such unlikely places as Mexico and Argentina. It seems, however, that wherever Egyptological research starts, it will at some point or other need to wend its way to Brooklyn.

**The library's great value is that so many things are concentrated in one place. The result is one-stop shopping for scholars.**

# A Salvador Dali, Hanging in Rikers Island

**An original work by Salvador Dali** hangs in the lobby of a jail on Rikers Island. It's a depiction of the Crucifixion, done in what appears to be crayon with splashes of ink on plain brown paper, the sort of paper the butcher uses to wrap meat. But it's a Dali all right—original and authentic.

There are several legends around why Dali made the drawing. The story heard most is that the artist's son was arrested and brought to Rikers Island, where he was treated well. To show his gratitude, Dali arranged to come out and visit the inmates one day, but he became ill and couldn't make the trip. Instead, he stayed in his New York hotel room and dashed off the drawing, which his wife, the famously imperious Gala, then brought to the island and donated to the prisoners.

The only thing wrong with the story is that Dali had no children. He wasn't all that good at showing gratitude, either. What really happened is that a reform-minded correction commissioner, Anna Moscowitz Kross, an advocate of art as rehabilitative therapy, arranged for Dali to come meet with the many "artist inmates" at Rikers. A very well-publicized visit was arranged, but the artist did become ill on the day of the appointment. So he dashed off the Crucifixion and sent it in his stead.

It wasn't always in the lobby. Originally, the work hung in the prisoners' dining room, its intended location. But the dining room was not a good or safe place for the Dali. Some say the drawing was too near the slop sink where inmates scraped leftovers from trays. Others say the drawing became a target during food fights and other "disturbances" in the dining room, back in the days when Rikers Island was a synonym for trouble. A *New York Times* story in 2001 blamed the removal of the picture on a direct hit by a coffee cup, which shattered the glass.

**There are several legends around why Dali made the drawing. The story heard most is that the artist's son was arrested and brought to Rikers Island, where he was treated well. The only thing wrong with the story is that Dali had no children.**

Whatever the reason, the Dali was certainly damaged. Something that appears to be coffee stains, and tracks of red Kool-Aid, have dripped down the picture, and there is water damage along the bottom. It's also unclear whether that splash of ink in the center of the crucifix is food fight damage or artistic genius.

By 1986, the drawing was out of the dining room and in a wooden crate behind a sofa at Department of Corrections headquarters in downtown Manhattan. At some point, someone opened the crate and took a look at what was inside, and it was decided to have the work appraised.

The results of the appraisal were staggering. Dali was still alive; he

lived until 1989. Yet the "dashed-off" work was appraised at anywhere from $150,000 to $250,000.

To a city agency on a tight budget, a quick hit of a quarter of a million must have looked very appealing indeed. But cooler heads prevailed, and the picture was reframed in a highly protective double-glazed case and then hung on the lobby wall.

It isn't the first thing your eye catches. The picture hangs in the Eric M. Taylor section of Rikers. Straight ahead as you walk into Taylor is the first of the cagelike walls of bars that remind a visitor he's in a jail. To the right is the sealed room in which all weapons must be checked. The Dali hangs alone and out of the way, on the wall to the left, its glass catching the glare of overhead fluorescent lights. Guards hurry past. Security checks buzz. A poster proclaiming TOTAL EFFICIENCY ACCOUNTABILITY MANAGEMENT SYSTEM fights for attention.

But step back a bit, out of the glare, and you can see the picture as it was meant to be seen. Then it becomes something of a negative—the cross is the light part of the image, the background the dark, just the kind of surrealist "trick" one might expect of Dali.

Not everybody passes it by without noticing it. David Goodman is the warden of the Eric M. Taylor Center. He first served there in 1982 as a young correction officer, and he remembers the Dali, although at the time, he didn't realize what it was. But warden Goodman says he now spends "a good part of my day looking at the picture and thinking about it." Goodman has become fascinated by Dali, he says, and he has explored as much of the artist's work as he can find.

As for the "artist inmates" who were supposed to have found rehabilitative values in the Dali picture, they don't get to see it. And there are artist inmates, Goodman says—"truly talented people." They

**Something that appears to be coffee stains, and tracks of red Kool-Aid, have dripped down the picture, and there is water damage along the bottom. It's also unclear whether that splash of ink in the center of the crucifix is food fight damage or artistic genius.**

are given pastels and paper, which they use for elaborate drawings. Many make soap carvings, not with a knife to be sure, but by wetting the soap and molding it with their hands.

Outside the jail, on a clear spring day, a visitor is strikingly aware of the spaciousness of the 415-acre island, the wonderful views of Manhattan. A plane passes overhead, heading down to LaGuardia Airport for a landing. One wonders how many people flying into LaGuardia would know that this lovely island is a prison.

Precious few. And fewer still are aware that a work of art by Salvador Dali, dedicated to its inmates, hangs in that prison, either.

## ■ A Sculpture Garden Grows in Queens

**In a city where space is at a premium,** where developers fight greedily over vacant lots strewn with broken glass and debris, and where the city fathers have been known to bulldoze community gardens in favor of high-rises, the idea of a public city park for large-scale sculpture sounds like an audacious and ludicrous impossibility.

But there is one—and it's a beaut. Along the western edge of Queens, where the East River splits around Roosevelt Island, on four and a half acres of grassy space utterly open to sky and waterway, sits Socrates Sculpture Park.

There's nothing else remotely like it in the city or even close by. An hour or so up the Hudson or two hours down into New Jersey are sculpture museums that exhibit works outdoors. But neither is a public park, and neither is an outdoor studio, as Socrates is, where artists can work in the setting in which their work will be shown.

Socrates is, as its mission statement says, "the only site in the New York Metropolitan area specifically dedicated to providing artists with opportunities to create and exhibit large-scale sculpture and multimedia projects in an outdoor environment that invites interaction between artists, artworks and the public."

That's a mouthful, but it's exactly what Socrates' creators intended, and it's exactly what the two women currently in charge of the park, executive director Alyson Baker and programs manager Robyn Donohue, make happen year-round. It's also a place where people from the surrounding community can and do walk their dogs, have a barbecue, hold hands, or just chill out on the grass, watching the boats go by, with the view of Manhattan across the way.

**Along the western edge of Queens, where the East River splits around Roosevelt Island, on four and a half acres of grassy space utterly open to sky and waterway, sits Socrates Sculpture Park.**

**This creation of art on the spot, in the open, accessible to all, is part of what makes the park not just a place for display but also a laboratory of public art.**

The garden is the brainchild of sculptor Mark di Suvero, whose large-scale sculptures made from steel girders are housed in museums around the world. Di Suvero's studio overlooks a space that had once been a marine terminal.

But obsolescence had led to neglect, and by the 1980s, all di Suvero could see out his window was an illegal dumping ground that was probably toxic and definitely dangerous. In 1985, he put together a coalition of other artists, community residents, and volunteers. For a year, the group worked to clean up the mess and plant grass and trees. Their efforts had a ripple effect. Funds were raised, arts programming got under way, and in due course, the abandoned garbage dump was reclaimed and became a sculpture park.

In 1993, Socrates came under the jurisdiction of the city's Parks and Recreation department, and in 1998, it was officially assigned as parkland. Its name does homage to both the Greek philosopher and to the people of Astoria, the heart of New York's Greek community.

Much of the materials used in the park are donated by building supply businesses in the neighborhood or by an organization that matches materials no longer needed with people who might need them. It all gets used, if not by the artists creating work on the site, then by the people taking art classes here—especially the kids, who pile in for art-making sessions to the tune of 60 to 80 per day in July and August.

This creation of art on the spot, in the open, accessible to all, is part of what makes the park not just a place for display but also a laboratory of public art. "Other places encourage public art," Alyson Baker says, "but this is unique."

Watch Peter Kreider and some grounds

workers create Derby Dusting. Kreider is a grantee of Socrates' Emerging Artists program, while the grounds workers helping him have been recruited through the Works Initiative Program, which trains and employs residents from the nearby Astoria and Queensbridge public housing projects. Kreider's work is a maze built of roadway material. In fact, on one level, it is a roadway. Kreider has scaled it one half-inch to a foot and will paint double yellow lines and crosswalks on it in appropriate places. But he will also map out a fingerprint with it—a stylized version, belonging to no particular individual finger. There's both whimsy and gravity in the conception, growing here in this unlikely garden for art on the shores of Queens.

# Shooting Movies Where Bread Once Baked

**When Sarah Jessica Parker,** as *Sex and the City*'s Carrie Bradshaw, sashays past the Manolo Blahniks in the hallway-turned-closet of her Greenwich Village apartment, she's actually in a space where freshly baked bread and doughnuts were once shipped to stores around New York.

Tony Soprano's office in the back room of the Bada Bing! once held huge baking ovens.

Wendy's commercials are shot in what used to be the wrapping room, where the finished loaves were tucked into stay-fresh wrappings.

And what were once steam boxes, where the shaped dough was allowed to rise into loaves, are today dressing rooms to the stars.

It all takes place at Silvercup Studios, just over the bridge from midtown Manhattan in Queens.

When people think of New York and movies, they tend to think of

Tony Soprano's office in the back room of the Bada Bing! once held huge baking ovens. And what were once steam boxes, where the shaped dough was allowed to rise into loaves, are today dressing rooms to the stars.

exterior shots that capture the city's grittiness. But the city is home to significant production studios, too; in fact, New York's moviemaking tradition predates Hollywood's, and many of the industry's techniques and rituals were developed on back lots in Queens.

By the same token, most people believe that New York is a place where old buildings are routinely torn down to make way for the new. It ain't necessarily so. Sometimes, old buildings are simply given new life, a new purpose, and a new meaning, even when they keep the old name.

The yellow brick building that takes up a city block at the base of the Queensboro Bridge started life in the 1920s as the home of Silvercup bread, "The World's Finest," as it styled itself on the legendary red sign atop the building. The building was built "to be a baking machine,"

**"We're a hotel for the whole business," says Stuart Suna. "We basically rent out rooms, and our room service is lights, lumber, and paint."**

says Joe Szabo, the plant manager, who has been caring for the building since he joined the staff as an assistant engineer in 1962. The bread it produced was 100 percent pure, made with no preservatives, and the company was the proud sponsor of the *Lone Ranger* television show, a staple of kids' TV viewing in the 1950s.

Silvercup stopped baking on the site in 1975, although it is still in the bread-making business. Businessman Harry Suna bought the building in 1979 to house a sheet-metal company. But the sheet-metal operation took up only 35,000 square feet of the building's 240,000 square feet, so Suna and his sons Stuart and Alan, both trained as architects, looked around for something else to do with the space.

They considered tennis courts—both Suna boys loved the sport—housing, and industry. But the city, hoping to lure filmmakers back to New York, was offering incentives for production studios at the time, so the Sunas decided to give that a try.

No one in the family knew the first thing about film production, says Stuart Match Suna, who runs Silvercup with his brother, Alan, but when the first studio they opened in 1983 became an instant hit, booked all the time, they quickly learned—enough to become the

**No wonder Woody Allen chose Silvercup to make *Broadway Danny Rose* and *Purple Rose of Cairo.* Or Spike Lee for *Do the Right Thing.***

largest independent, full-service film and television production facility in the Northeast.

"We're a hotel for the whole business," says Stuart Suna. "We basically rent out rooms, and our room service is lights, lumber, and paint." It means that while HBO, for example, brings in its own talent—writers, actors, designers—and builds the sets in the studios it uses with its own labor, the lumber for building the sets, the paint for making them "real," and the lighting used in shooting are all available on the premises. Suna calls the result "affordable studios," easier and cheaper than renting or buying raw space and having to furnish it with everything needed—and only minutes from midtown Manhattan.

No wonder Woody Allen chose Silvercup to make *Broadway Danny Rose* and *Purple Rose of Cairo.* Or Spike Lee for *Do the Right Thing.*

But you don't have to be a "New York" director to choose to produce here. From movies like *Mr. Deeds* to *Stuart Little 2* to *Romancing the Stone* and *Crocodile Dundee II . . .* from commercials for Wendy's or Old Navy or Victoria's Secret . . . from the music videos for Whitney Houston, Janet Jackson, and Bon Jovi—to name just a few—to fashion shoots for *Vogue, Elle,* and *Mirabella . . .* and of course, for *The Sopranos* and the women and men of *Sex and the City* and other television shows, everyone enjoys the chance to shoot in New York.

And when they want bread or doughnuts, they just order out.

For decades, New York turned its back on its waterfront, leaving it to seagulls, hardy ducks, and a host of—let's face it—rather grubby-looking industries.

# A City on Water

NEW YORK IS A CITY SURROUNDED BY WATER, but until recently, this gift of nature held little interest for most New Yorkers. For decades, New York turned its back on its waterfront, leaving it to seagulls, hardy ducks, and a host of—let's face it—rather grubby-looking industries.

In one of those sea changes that take place in a culture, for reasons both concrete and ephemeral, that tide is turning. Today, millions of New Yorkers are demonstrating their raised consciousness of living in a city on water. Some are giving up park views from their apartments and forking out big dollars for river or harbor views. Some stand patiently with a fishing rod, casting a line into a newly clean Hudson River. Others own boats—fabulous yachts or tiny dinghies. Some live on boats.

More and more, New Yorkers are commuting by water. And, no matter how many years they have been doing it, they put down their newspaper as the boat pulls into its slip and gaze up again for a glimpse, perennially fresh, of the New York skyline.

## Want to Build a Boat? Call Floating the Apple

No one typifies this littoral consciousness more than a group of water-loving New Yorkers who call themselves Floating the Apple. Sometime in the 1990s, some key members of this group looked out at all that water around the city and began thinking about ways to get on it easily and inexpensively. Not just get on it themselves; they wanted to offer the mind-clearing freshness of a day sailing or rowing to other New Yorkers, especially children.

Their solution: a graceful but almost extinct vessel called a Whitehall gig.

Whitehall gigs have a noble history on the Hudson. They are open, four-oared rowboats, 25 feet long, sail-equipped, sleek, jaunty, and fast. In the early days of the city's commercial shipping, they were a common sight in the harbor, meeting incoming vessels, carrying messages, delivering and gathering news. But by the time Floating the Apple started to look for one, they had disappeared from New York. The only one then on the market was in the United Kingdom, priced at $22,000.

For that kind of money, the group determined to build its own. Don Betts, a Floating the Apple member, recalls how it all got started: "One week, we had nothing but a roomful of enthusiastic people and a decision to re-create the Whitehall gig. No space to call our own, no tools, nothing. Then someone donated space, and someone else donated a shop full of tools, and before you know it, we had everything we needed to start a boatbuilding program."

The choice of the gig was not merely sentimental. With its big-boat watertight bulkheads, its built-in foam flotation, and its provision for a coxswain, the Whitehall gig offered a level of safety and a chance for teamwork that was ideal for a kid-oriented program. So right out of the chute, Floating the Apple hooked up with a nearby middle school that had an interest in the Hudson River. Work got under way in the donated space on March 1, 1994. The boat was in the water by September of that year.

After that, they just kept going, working with other schools, including one of the city's most exclusive private prep schools and one of its toughest public high schools. In fact, the two teamed up to build a Whitehall gig. Emotionally disturbed kids from another school also built one. A crew from a school for kids classified as at risk spent five

**Whitehall gigs have a noble history on the Hudson. They are open, four-oared rowboats, 25 feet long, sail-equipped, sleek, jaunty, and fast.**

months building a gig. Today, schools that encourage what the Board of Education calls "external, experiential education" offer internships for helping to build the gigs. In budget-strapped New York, the group constantly struggles for funds, most of them coming from a patchwork of private sources.

Mike Davis, another Floating the Apple member, says the kids learn the art of building with lightning speed and "make it into a special interaction that breaks all bonds," separate from school and family. "They come in and create their world," Davis says, "and you never have to say 'Don't!' to them." For many, the comeback of the Whitehall gig has been the catalyst for personal comebacks as well. As of this writing, New York City schoolkids have built 16 Whitehall gigs and are working on their seventeenth and eighteenth. All are built for the use of the public at large.

But building the boats is only part of it. The kids also maintain the boats, clean and repair them. And of course, they row them, learn coxswain skills in them, compete in them. At the boathouses Floating the Apple runs around the city—on the Hudson in Manhattan, on the East River in Brooklyn, at Hunts Point in the Bronx, and on the Harlem River separating Manhattan from the Bronx—neighborhood folks and anyone who just happens to drop in have the same chance to go boating, learn boating, help out with boatbuilding.

**New York City schoolkids have built 16 Whitehall gigs and are working on their seventeenth and eighteenth. All are built for the use of the public at large.**

Ask Becky Olinger, who chanced on some literature about the group. Olinger had canoed as a kid but didn't know of any way to get onto the water in New York City. She contacted Floating the Apple, and someone told her to come on down to Pier 84 on the Hudson River.

She did, and "I was hooked," Olinger says. "It's addictive." She went rowing every week thereafter. On winter evenings and weekends, she works on the boatbuilding, and she's there for the launch parties and the regularly scheduled community rowing and sailing. She leads trips, too, including the rowboat flotilla that accompanies the annual swim around Manhattan in June.

So New York's waters, the city's "largest public space and richest wildlife preserve," as Floating the Apple boasts, are once again alive with Whitehall gigs. Take a look any fair summer Wednesday or Sunday. See them rowing from Red Hook to Horns Hook up the East River, or from the Hudson boathouses to Governors Island. Historic boats once again plying the city's waters.

## The Sea Captain Who Ferries Commuters

**John Willette looks like everybody's idea of a sea captain,** burly-framed and with a weather-lightened beard. And he has the savvy and experience to go along with the looks.

Willette was born not far from the major port of a seafaring nation, Scotland. He first crossed the Atlantic Ocean at the age of six months, then grew up in Queens, a borough bordered by rivers and bays. He served in the Navy, the Coast Guard, the merchant fleet, and on an offshore oil-field supply boat.

Eventually there came a time when Willette wanted to stop

**The East River is no simple waterway.**
**It has a heavy current and swells as high as two feet,**
**plenty high for the landlubbers Willette is transporting.**

traveling and come home, but that didn't mean he wanted to be on dry land. That is why today he is the skipper of a Sea Otter ferryboat that sails Manhattan's East River and Upper New York Bay. Employed since 1993 by New York Waterways, the company that pioneered the return of commercial passenger boat traffic to New York, he has driven boats of every size on waterways around the city. But the East River is his bailiwick, whether he is taking investment bankers to Wall Street or baseball fans to Shea Stadium.

The East River, which is indeed east (of Manhattan) but is a tidal strait, not a river, is no simple waterway. It has a heavy current and swells as high as two feet, plenty high for the landlubbers Willette is transporting. Add to that the other traffic heading up and down the narrow channel, and captaining a ferry of any size takes a real seaman. The 97-passenger Otter, manned by the captain and a single deckhand, travels at 35 to 40 miles per hour, making it from the bottom of Wall Street to 90th Street on Manhattan's East Side, a distance of some seven miles—in 15 minutes. And that includes stopping at 34th Street to discharge and pick up passengers.

For the passengers, commuters, shoppers, and anyone who wants to avoid traffic congestion and/or the subway, it's a beautiful and pleasant way to travel. The protected cabin has windows all around, so you can watch the towers of Manhattan to one side or the low-rise industry of Brooklyn and Queens. You can see helicopters take off and land, try to peer into the apartments on Roosevelt Island, or get a feel for how nice it might be to become mayor and live in Gracie Mansion.

And, lest you think that going up and down the East River would lead to ennui for the captain, rest assured. "There is something new on the river every day," Willette says. A couch one day, a picnic table another, and the occasional "floater," a human corpse among the flotsam and jetsam of the river.

One hot July evening, Willette saw what looked like a dead whale in the river. As he headed toward it, somebody waved. The whale turned out to be an overturned party boat. Thirty-eight people were adrift, ten of them in the boat's sole life raft, the others clinging to the overturned hull. Willette called in a Mayday, rigged a rescue ladder, and had taken five people aboard his vessel by the time the police rescue craft arrived.

On September 11, 2001, a day when New York Waterways boats moved 160,000 people out of harm's way, John Willette evacuated

**On September 11, 2001, a day when New York Waterways boats moved 160,000 people out of harm's way, John Willette evacuated people from Manhattan to the New Jersey side of the Hudson River.**

people from Manhattan to the New Jersey side of the Hudson River. In the days following, he ferried rescue workers to and from Ground Zero. Weeks later, he helped bring families of the fallen to the site. Two of the ferries on Willette's East River run are named for victims of that day: the *Father Mychal Judge* and the *Moira Smith,* in honor respectively of the Fire Department chaplain and the police officer, the sole female officer, killed in the World Trade Center collapse. These are boats for which Willette and the deckhands who ride with him have a special feeling.

## Harbor Pilots: Don't Try to Dock Your Ship Without Them

**No major vessel, or one flying a foreign flag,** may enter or leave New York harbor on its own. By law, it must be guided into or out of the harbor by a harbor pilot, specifically, by one of the 80-plus pilots of the New York and New Jersey Sandy Hook Pilots Association. Only they have the knowledge and expertise needed to maneuver ships through New York's tricky harbor, one of the busiest in the world.

It is the occupation of a true elite. Harbor pilots are highly trained, rigorously tested before being entrusted with a ship, and held to strict standards throughout their careers. They are also welcome sights to weary ship captains and crews, who gratefully help the pilots aboard their ships, and turn over to them the job of negotiating New York's waters to bring ship, crew, and cargo safely to berth.

Under the circumstances, it's no wonder that those who achieve the status of pilot dress in suits and ties when they go to work. In fact, until the end of the Roaring Twenties, the pilot's dress code included a top hat!

Captain Bill Sherwood, president of the New York arm of the

association, seems the perfect exemplar of everybody's idea of a New York harbor pilot: straight-backed and elegant in his cuff-linked shirt and tightly knotted tie, comfortable with the authority he holds, articulate to the point of eloquence. A veteran pilot himself, he explains the training each pilot must go through: seven years as a deputy, "piloting vessels of the lowest reasonable tonnage and draft, then working your way up in increments to the top grade of branch pilot." Passing the federal and the more stringent New York State piloting exams requires knowledge of hydrology, navigation, systems management, and more.

It also requires that the pilot-candidate reproduce from memory the 24 charts that plot the area the pilots cover, from Manhattan to Albany, from New Jersey to Rhode Island, the harbor itself, and all the rivers and streams that flow into it.

**Captain Bill Sherwood seems the perfect exemplar of everybody's idea of a New York harbor pilot: straight-backed and elegant, comfortable with the authority he holds, articulate to the point of eloquence.**

A candidate who flunks the exam gets a single second chance. Unlike the bar exam for lawyers, which can be taken again and again until a candidate passes, this is pilotage. If you flunk a second time, you're out.

Pilots, you see, had earned that top hat.

Pilots start each job by jumping out of a damp, heaving launch and climbing hand over hand up a rope ladder onto the deck of a freighter, tanker, or liner. Once aboard the destination vessel, the pilot steps to the bridge, shakes hands with the captain, gets filled in on the vessel's particulars—size, engine, mast height, any problems. The pilot then provides courses and orders while the quartermaster steers the vessel in response.

It takes some three to four hours to move a ship from a Manhattan pier to sea, and about three hours the other way, one of the shorter exits or dockings in the harbor. During that time, the pilot is bringing to bear all his training and experience, all the charts in his head plus his gut feel for the geography, the tides, the winds, the weather. The vessel that he is piloting is carrying valuable cargo, like the freighters that transport the oil that warms the Northeast in winter. It may also be carrying hazardous or toxic material, or a group of vacationing passengers. Its crew and officers may represent many nations and languages and many levels of seamanship.

But no matter how competent the ship's leadership, no expertise on open water is a match for what a vessel must contend with when it comes close to shore.

**Along the way, the pilot is directing the vessel around rocks, reefs, and shoals, down narrow channels and around sharp turns, working against strong tidal currents and contending with the traffic all around him.**

New York harbor is so protected as to be almost camouflaged. An incoming vessel approaches through two fingers of land that form a natural gateway—Sandy Hook on the New Jersey side, and Long Island on the New York side. Then it veers north through the Narrows, past Staten Island, into the quiescence of Upper New York Bay, then straight up either side of Manhattan, or around the back of Staten Island, or along the Brooklyn waterfront.

Along the way, the pilot is directing the vessel around rocks, reefs, and shoals, down narrow channels and around sharp turns, working against strong tidal currents and contending with the traffic all around him. In any weather. Whatever the visibility. Making decisions and taking actions in a New York minute, sometimes in a New York split second.

Consider, says Bill Sherwood, that you might have two ships, each 700 to 900 feet in length, both trying to enter a 600-foot-wide channel at the same moment. The pilots make sure it doesn't happen. Or you have a vessel that draws 48 feet when the Ambrose Channel, main waterway into the harbor, is 45 feet deep. The pilot knows how long the ship will have to wait for the tide or how much cargo must be lightered off the vessel to enable passage.

The job over—the vessel berthed or safely out to sea—it's back down the rope ladder to the launch. Another challenge. Imagine a ship the size of the U.S. Capitol building in length, some eight-story cruise ship with decks full of hotel rooms and swimming pools. Or maybe a floating garage stowing 8000 cars. While the sea pitches and rolls under the launch, while the vessel steams ahead at 10 to 14 knots, while the wind blows and the waves tickle his toes, the pilot clambers down rung by rung.

In the waiting launch, the deckhand is counting the rungs, assessing distance, time, and the height of the swells.

"Stop!" the deckhand will instruct, judging that the next swell will raise the launch high enough for the pilot to jump backwards into it. Pilot Sherwood has never taken a fall into the drink from a ladder, but it does happen to even the most agile pilots.

Sherwood tells the story of a pilot launch hit by seas so ferocious that it rolled over and, astonishingly, righted itself. Two pilots were aboard the launch at the time. When they returned safely to port, one of them quit on the spot. The other is a New York harbor pilot to this day.

## On a Tugboat in New York Harbor
## They May Be Little, but They're Tough

**Captain Dan Ramsey** peers out from his aerie in the wheelhouse of the *Joan Turecamo,* high above the deck and the water. From the lofty wheelhouse, he has a sweeping bird's-eye view of the scene around his boat, open sky, gulls swooping. Like any captain, he is the absolute master of his ship, small though that ship may be.

Dan Ramsey is the captain of a tugboat, a vessel that, in the seafaring world, is something like the Katharine Hepburn character in *Pat and Mike.* As Spencer Tracy put it: "There ain't much meat on her, but what there is is 'cherce.'"

Ramsey's tug is part of the Moran fleet, those little boats with the big white M's on their smokestacks that are all over the city's waterways. At 4290 horsepower, the twin-screw vessel is compact, built for power and efficiency. But compact as it may be, each crew member has his own stateroom, and the galley is well-stocked for the two-week stint onboard that each crew serves. There are books to read, videos to watch, and space in which to be alone, if you choose. It is almost, well, cozy.

But Ramsey and his four-man crew—mate Bill Morris, chief engineer Anthony Amendola, and deckhands Sam Coolidge and James Hennessy—don't spend much time lounging. Most of the time they're working, doing what tugboats do: pushing, or sometimes pulling, other ships, bringing them home to dock. They push tankers, scows, barges, freighters, cargo vessels, ships that, as Ramsey says, "are designed to get from point A to point B, period. They're not really able to dock on their own." Sometimes tugboats are on hand to nudge home those big passenger liners, too. While most contemporary cruise ships have thrusters that propel them right into a pier, tugboats may stand by for safety's sake.

But it's in bringing home the tankers and freighters that tugs earn their money. A tug meets its vessel out in the bay. The little boat sidles up to the massive one—some more than 400 feet long—

**Compact as it may be, each crew member has his own stateroom, and the galley is well-stocked for the two-week stint onboard that each crew serves.**

DORIS MORAN

and slips its nose into a notch in the stern. At this point, a pilot may also be onboard, depending on the nature of the ship. The tug secures itself by cable, then nudges the massive vessel this way and that, nosing the larger ship through the bay and whatever other waterways stand between it and its destination. They may be headed through the narrows to Staten Island to dock a container ship, or bringing a tanker full of fuel oil up the Hudson to Albany.

Once in the vicinity of its pier, the tug nestles it in just right. To dock a large, heavily loaded ship, two or even three tugboats may be needed, working in close coordination with each other, the crew, and the pilot. In rough weather, the tug may pull its charge rather than tug it, keeping a reasonable distance from the other, heaving vessel.

Winter is the busiest time. All those oil tankers carrying heating fuel to keep New Yorkers warm must be brought safely in. But whatever the season, Moran's tugs work 365 days a year, 24/7.

The job they do is harder than it looks, and a lot can go wrong. Think of the consequences of smashing an oil-laden tanker into a city pier or losing a cargo of frozen meat in the Hudson River. Regulations are strict, and training and licensing are rigorous. To earn his captain's stripes, Ramsey trained with the Coast Guard, then worked on tugs for several decades. Engineer Amendola is a graduate of the New York Merchant Marine Academy. You can also work your way up from deckhand, as AB (Able-Bodied seaman) Sam Coolidge intends to do.

Tugboats are the eternal bridesmaids of maritime New York, always there, paving the way. They have figured prominently in the city's, even the nation's, history. It was tugboats that led the parade of ships for the unveiling of the Statue of Liberty in 1886. Moran tugs supported the D-Day landings of World War II, hauling portable docking facilities for supply ships to Normandy. Tugboats escorted the limping *Stockholm* into port in 1956, its bow smashed to a snub-nosed mess after its collision with the *Andrea Doria,* its survivors huddled on its deck. We see tugs all the time, chugging up the Hudson on workday mornings, spraying streams of water for our delight on the Fourth of July. They are the eternal supporting players of New York's port, supplying the muscle, making the harbor stars look good.

**The job they do is harder than it looks, and a lot can go wrong. Think of the consequences of smashing an oil-laden tanker into a city pier or losing a cargo of frozen meat in the Hudson River.**

Look out your window anytime in the middle of the
night in New York, and you'll see lights on somewhere.

# Sleepless in New York

**N**EW YORK IS THE CITY THAT NEVER SLEEPS. For some
people, that means a glamorous night on the town—hobnobbing
with the rich and famous. But to many other New Yorkers,
nighttime is when they get up and go to work. The city's pace may
slow in the wee hours, but it doesn't cease. Look out your window
anytime in the middle of the night in New York, and you'll see
lights on somewhere, cars on the street. You'll hear a laugh, a
shout, the grinding sound of a sanitation truck, a car alarm going
off—maddeningly—because somebody is walking by.

## Hunts Point,
## The City's All-Night Giant Vegetable Stand

**"I got a hundred boxes. They're twenty dollars."**

"Eighteen."

"No. Twenty."

"Awright. Make it two boxes."

Arthur DePinto of the produce packing company Krisp-Pak deftly
keys in the order on a computer recessed in the glass-enclosed office:
two green pepper. The price is figured automatically. "What else?"
DePinto asks his customer.

"How much romaine?" the customer wants to know.

Like a great many of Krisp-Pak's customers, like a great many of
the buyers and sellers at the Hunts Point Market tonight and every
night, the customer is Korean-born, and his English lacks a certain
idiomatic fluency. DePinto is accustomed to the speech pattern,
however, and understands that his customer, by now an acquaintance
of many years, is asking the price of the romaine, not how much of it
there is.

"Twelve," DePinto answers.

The customer wrinkles his nose, shakes his head. He scans his

order sheet, a preprinted list representing the produce needs of a number of Korean delis and restaurants around the city. "You got kirby?" he asks.

The Hunts Point Terminal Market, to give it its proper name, moves nearly three billion pounds of produce a year, generating revenues in excess of $1.5 billion, more than any other terminal market in the world. The market it serves—supermarket chains, restaurants, street vendors, in the Greater New York area—contains more than 15 million people and constitutes perhaps the most ethnically diverse region in the world. It is a cooperative, owned and operated by its wholesalers.

The market sits on nearly 200 acres in the Bronx, on a point of land—Hunts Point—that juts out between the East River and the Bronx River. The area around the market is filled with small, one-story factories or repair shops that are closed and dark at night. The market is self-contained, fenced in, its entrances and exits guarded. Restaurant eating and takeout are available on-site; there's no need to leave the market area—and no place to go if you do.

**The Hunts Point Terminal Market moves nearly three billion pounds of produce a year, generating revenues in excess of 1.5 billion dollars.**

163

Hunts Point is a good place to be sleepless in New York. It is open straight through the week except for Saturdays.

Most of the market's acreage is given over to railroad tracks and parking for the army of vans, small trucks, and cars driven by the customers and workers. About 35 acres are occupied by the market's buildings, four long avenues of sheds with loading docks on either side. Tractor-trailer trucks back up to these loading docks to off-load produce from around the country: California, New Jersey, the Midwest. Or to load up on produce from the interior stalls occupied by Krisp-Pak and the 50-plus other wholesalers of the market.

Hunts Point is a good place to be sleepless in New York. It is open straight through the week except for Saturdays, starting at 9 p.m. on Sunday night and going straight through Friday. The buying and selling do stop at midday, giving time for restocking and cleanup, before resuming again at nine or ten at night. And while the facilities are state-of-the-art, with high-tech refrigerated buildings and computerized inventory, this is still the land of the forklift and the hand truck and brawny members of Teamsters Local 202 delivering the goods.

To a visitor, the atmosphere appears to fall somewhere between the intrigue of an Asian bazaar and the high finance of a commodities market trading floor—all carried out in an open-air setting seasoned by the fragrance of fresh fruits and vegetables.

The first buyers in, says Krisp-Pak's John Garcia, are the chain store buyers. They're there by 10 p.m., buying in bulk. The last to arrive are the peddlers. "They want to see what people are stuck with," says Garcia, "so they come late." Everybody else is there all the time, checking prices, negotiating, looking for the best deal.

Bob Rathgeb, a produce buyer for a New Jersey chain of markets, typically starts taking orders from his customers at two thirty in the afternoon. He gets to the market fairly early. Then he's up and down the avenues of stalls, checking the goods, keeping track of prices. Sometimes he buys an item, then finds it for a cheaper price at another packer's stall. What does he do? "I try to renegotiate," he says. He goes back to where he bought it, tells them he found the same thing for a dime cheaper down

the way. Maybe they'll give it to him for that price, maybe they won't.

There's a wholesaler's side to this, too. "There's stuff I want to move now because I know there's more coming in tomorrow," Arthur DePinto says. "Or maybe there's nothing coming later, so I don't budge on the price."

That's the other thing: Different nights of the week feature different products. Tonight at Krisp-Pak, for example, the trucks from California are in: artichokes in various sizes, broccoli, carrots, lettuces, mesclun, romaine, scallions, spinach. There's also a shipment of superb honeydew. Arthur has sliced one open in the office; he's urging customers to try it, then buy some.

"It's a rat race," says Bob Rathgeb, "and it's always a challenge." The atmosphere, he contends, manages to be both cutthroat and familial—a fierce competitive battle within a connected kind of tribal unit.

To John Garcia, the market is something else as well. He sees it as "a processing center for immigrants." Ever since the market began back in the 1880s, Garcia contends, "it has provided people with no English and no skills a means of providing for their family. Today," he says, "it's the Koreans who have revitalized the market with their energy and their resourcefulness. It lets them live the American dream in their lifetime, lets their kids become lawyers and doctors. This," he concludes, "is the secret of the market."

Maybe. Or maybe its secret is that the people who work here, in this upside-down, day-for-night world in a part of the city that is otherwise utterly deserted at night, love being here.

**Ever since the market began back in the 1880s, Garcia contends, "it has provided people with no English and no skills a means of providing for their family. It lets them live the American dream in their lifetime, lets their kids become lawyers and doctors."**

# Crusing the Streets With a Late-Night Cabdriver

**The difference between driving a taxi** in New York by day and at night, says longtime taxi driver Bill C., is as stark a contrast as—well, night and day.

Bill sums it up this way: "During the day, people are buttoned-up, in a hurry, focused on a goal. At night, they're out to play. They relax. The pressure is off. They say things they would never say during the day. They do things they would never do during the day."

Here's how Bill breaks it down. "From 10 p.m. to midnight, you get the good people, the people who went to dinner, saw a show, maybe stopped for a drink, and now they're on their way home. From midnight on, God only knows what you get."

Bill has gotten it all. A cabbie since 1975, he has seen the best and

TAXI FARE

$2.00 Initial Charge

30¢ Per ⅕ Mile

20¢ Per Minute Stopped or Slow Traffic

50¢ Night Surcharge

worst of human behavior—and just about everything in between. His taxi's back seat has been a confessional, a boudoir, a fight arena, a theater of farce. It has held everyone from an elderly woman who asked Bill to wait while she rather obviously purchased illegal drugs from a youthful dealer, to a well-known pastor who blurted out that his son had just committed suicide and that he believed it was his fault.

"That was a tough ride," says Bill.

On one terrifying occasion, he drove a guy who put a gun to Bill's head and demanded his money and his car keys. Bill gave him both.

Not infrequently, he says, he drives ardent young couples who "suddenly get quiet like a church." Bill, whose policy is to avoid looking in the rearview mirror unless

**Bill has gotten it all. A cabbie since 1975, he has seen the best and worst of human behavior—and just about everything in between. His taxi's back seat has been a confessional, a boudoir, a fight arena, a theater of farce.**

it's a safety issue, nevertheless notices that "heads disappear. A while later "one head pops up, then the other." Bill continues resolutely to keep his eye on the road.

"People tell you things," he says. He can't count the number of women who have vented their anger or sorrow over broken love affairs. Once, a young woman in tears asked Bill to drive her to the FDR Drive along the East River and to drop her anyplace between 23rd and 34th streets. On the way, she sobbed and told him she'd just been summarily dumped by her boyfriend.

She was distraught. Bill was nervous. The highway at that point offers direct access to the East River. He tried talking to her.

"You know," he said, "you're a very pretty woman. I bet if you put out the word tomorrow that you're available, your phone will start ringing off the hook." He pulled off the highway and stopped the cab and spent two hours talking to her, until finally she asked him to take her home.

For days after that, Bill scanned the newspapers to see if she had perhaps made her way to the river after all. But it appeared that getting her through the night had gotten her through the worst of her distress.

Bill likes driving a cab. "You accomplish something quickly," he says. "You get someone somewhere, give them a good ride. And people appreciate it—most of the time." Besides, he says, "I'm out; I feel free; I'm not confined to a room in a building that doesn't move. And the time flies by. It literally flies by, even when I'm stuck in traffic."

**After the third car passed and honked, Bill looked in his rearview mirror. His passenger had gone topless. She was naked from the waist up.**

Cruising at night, Bill listens to talk shows, sports, and news on the radio. There was a time when the wee small hours of the morning brought out the bartenders and waiters heading for home. No more. Now it's all partygoers, barflies, people who've been dancing the night away in the clubs. One night, a woman got in the cab and gave a corner intersection as her destination. There's a mental game Bill likes to play: He tries to picture the destination he's driving to.

In this case, all that came into his mind was a nondescript retail shop, which he was sure would be closed at this hour, and a strip joint next door. He continued to drive. A car passed him and honked, and the driver waved somewhat wildly. A second car passed and honked, and both driver and passenger were laughing. Bill wondered if he was dragging something. After the third car passed and honked, Bill looked in his rearview mirror. His passenger had gone topless. She was naked from the waist up.

"I went kind of ballistic," Bill reports. "I asked her what the hell she thought she was doing." She told him she was a stripper, that she hadn't had time to rehearse at home, and so she was taking advantage of the cab ride to practice her act. Bill pulled over to the curb and told the stripper to get dressed and get out.

Bill leases his taxi medallion and the cab he drives from a broker who works for the ultimate owner of the medallion, an individual Bill does not know. The broker serves as middleman and takes care of all repairs and any problems. It's the best of both worlds, Bill says: the independence of ownership without its hassles.

He likes the city at night. He is endlessly intrigued by the parade of characters and the view of human character that nighttime driving affords him.

## Hanging Out in an All-Night Deli

**Who are the night owls** who make it worthwhile for corner delis to stay open all night long? Who hangs out in these oases of light in the dark Manhattan night? Are they really looking for a sandwich, a bottle of Tylenol? Can't the pantyhose purchase wait till daylight? Who really needs an ice cream at 4 a.m.?

Evidently, all sorts of New Yorkers do.

During the day, things are hopping at a small corner deli on the Upper West Side in Manhattan. The Korean-born staff who run the place seem to be able to ring up at least three customers at once, deftly

SLEEPLESS IN NEW YORK

bagging sandwiches and salads, dispensing with the breakfast, lunch, and after-work crowds.

At seven o'clock in the evening, the night shift takes over, moving in almost military fashion to their posts. Jong Soo, the night man, takes his place behind the register, his responsibility until seven the next morning. In the deli world, the man behind the cash register is the boss, and Jong Soo will be the de facto manager for the night. Karim heads to the deli counter, where he will stay all night, ready to make sandwiches. On stockroom and salad detail are Ed and Roberto, both Mexican immigrants. Ed makes sure the hot table and salad bar are full and that there are cold sodas and beer in the refrigerators. Roberto sits out in front of the store, near the flowers, where he peels vegetables for the salad bar and keeps an eye on the street life.

Pretty full staff for a quiet night.

Business remains steadily active till about midnight. Then the traffic subsides. The volume of people—and of noise—goes way down. The neighborhood and the city go to bed. For people who go to work in the morning, people with children in school, it's lights out.

But not for everybody.

There aren't many customers during the night, but a steady clientele nevertheless. At a little after 1 a.m., a taxi pulls up outside, and the cabbie saunters in, leaving his motor running. He fills a large cup with black coffee and, without pondering, grabs a packaged crumb cake and heads back to his rumbling cab. A woman wanders in for an ice cream.

At 2 a.m., a young man asks Karim for a ham and cheese sandwich—on rye. He looks bleary-eyed. It turns out he has been at the office until now, preparing a PowerPoint presentation for the boss, and he hasn't eaten since lunch. Since about six o'clock, however, he's been fantasizing about a ham and cheese sandwich, and now here it is.

At 3 a.m., the young woman who came in for ice cream at a little after 1 a.m. is back. By day, she writes speeches for a corporate executive. At night—sometimes all night—she works on a novel. Her apartment is just across from the deli, and when she gets stuck for

**At 2 a.m., a young man asks Karim for a ham and cheese sandwich on rye. He looks bleary-eyed. It turns out he has been at the office until now, preparing a PowerPoint presentation for the boss, and he hasn't eaten since lunch.**

ideas and stands up from her computer and looks out her window, the brightly lit deli is what she sees. She wanders over—for a package of rice sticks, a cup of coffee, and a little human interaction, hoping it will break the logjam in her mind.

A couple of firemen from the nearby firehouse walk in; they fill plastic containers with salad ingredients—surprisingly, perhaps, not with meat and potatoes. They have just been out on a call, and they're hungry.

At first light, three different trucks pull up and unload three different newspapers—the *Daily News,* the *Post,* the *Times.* Ed makes fresh coffee in both samovars, and waits. A bright-faced couple walks in. They are about to head out of town on a trip, due west across Interstate 80, and need some sustenance to get going. After they leave, things are quiet.

On a Saturday night, of course, it's very different. "Crazy," says Karim. People wander in all night, helping themselves to beer and sodas from the cooler, sometimes making the staff nervous. But the neighborhood is relatively safe, and so far there have been no incidents. Karim makes sandwich after sandwich; it's amazing how many people come home from a Saturday night dinner hungry. He prepares platters of cold cuts throughout the night for parties, after-parties, and—for the 3 a.m. or 4 a.m. calls—presumably, very private parties.

But even on Saturdays, things quiet down. Eventually 7 a.m. comes. The day shift takes over, and the first breakfasters of the morning start filtering into the deli. The long night is over, and New York is waking up.

**On a Saturday night, of course, it's very different. "Crazy," says Karim. People wander in all night, helping themselves to beer and sodas from the cooler, sometimes making the staff nervous.**

To many, it
seems a job out
of a romantic
film noir or an
Edward Hopper
painting.

**Night doorman in a Manhattan apartment tower.** To many, it seems a
job out of a romantic film noir or an Edward Hopper painting. It
speaks of dreamy possibilities—the chance to gather research for a
novel, to confront the life stories of fascinating "night people."

Actually, says Marty McDermott, who does the 10 p.m. to 6 a.m.
shift one night a week, it's mostly an opportunity to read the papers
from cover to cover, provided the building's insomniacs will let him.

McDermott's building is a large high-rise on the Upper West Side.
For the first hour or so of the night shift, he's pretty busy, holding the
door open for residents coming home after an evening out. By
midnight, however, the activity winds down. It's a weekday, after all.
People have to get up in the morning. McDermott goes to work, too,
peeling back the front page of the *Daily News* to find out what's going
on in the city.

It's not that nothing ever happens.

It's a big building, with a couple of thousand people. Somebody's
always traveling, somebody's plane is always late, somebody's always

## Night Doorman

arriving exhausted at three thirty in the morning with lots of luggage and a look of utter gratitude to have made it home.

Sometimes, yes, someone will roll in having had too much to drink. "It happens occasionally," McDermott says, "not often." The inebriate might need a little help getting into the elevator or, worse, might want to relate his life story.

Sometimes insomniacs do that, too; they wander down to the lobby, station themselves in front of the doorman's desk, and pour their hearts out. McDermott has learned to sit there and listen. After eight years on the job, he knows they'll tire eventually. Only once did he suggest to a resident that he go on back to bed. The guy, both an insomniac and a drinker, told the exact same life story every night.

There are no such problems on the day shift, which McDermott prefers—hands down. On the day shift, "you're always on the go, always doing something. You're getting the door, helping them with packages, dealing with the phones. It can get quite hectic." But that's good. "I like the action," McDermott says.

It's not surprising. McDermott is animated, friendly, with the ruddy face, quick smile, and readiness with words that often go along with being Irish in New York.

He likes his job. A New York native, he was born and raised in Manhattan, venturing to the Bronx for high school at Cardinal Hayes. He worked in an office for a while, but "I'm an outdoors person. I like getting out and moving around. I don't like to sit still." The night shift has too much sitting still.

But when something memorable does happen, it happens at night. Like the fire in the upper floors one winter night. With smoke filling the hallways and the source of the fire undiscovered, residents gathered in the lobby while the Fire Department checked it out. "Everyone remained calm," McDermott reports, even when the Fire Department, having declared the fire out, was called back to the building to deal with the smoke that continued to drift through the halls. It turned out that the fire was inside the outer wall of the building, burning slowly and

Sometimes insomniacs wander down to the lobby, station themselves in front of the doorman's desk, and pour their hearts out. McDermott has learned to sit there and listen.

steadily. Eventually, after much ruinous watering, it was quenched and the usual nighttime calm returned.

"They're very nice people, on the whole," says McDermott. But in a building this size, he's had to learn to deal with different personalities. Some of the personalities are cranky—people who complain that the doorman hasn't leaped up to open the door fast enough, or that he's not at his post ("Probably I'm helping someone else"). Some people— well, one person, well known as the building maniac—who calls the doorman "a jerk," or worse, at the drop of a hat. At least on the night shift, you don't have to put up with that.

177

**You won't find these things anywhere else—except as pale imitations. New York has the real thing.**

# Only in New York

**SOME THINGS HAPPEN ONLY IN NEW YORK.**
Either they happen here because New York is the kind of world capital that it is. Or New York is the kind of world capital it is because these things happen here. Either way, you won't find these things anywhere else—except as pale imitations. New York has the real thing.

## ■ Searching for Rockefeller Center's Christmas Tree

**Camera! Action! Lights!**

The Christmas tree at Rockefeller Center comes alive in a brilliant flash. Music plays; television cameras roll. Katie and Matt and the NBC crew carol out *Jingle Bells*. The Christmas season in New York has officially begun.

But even as this year's tree is welcomed, Dave Murbach is already thinking about next year's tree.

Murbach is the horticulturist who has been in charge of the legendary Christmas trees since the early 1980s. He actually goes on the road, beginning his search for the tree, not long after the previous year's tree has been taken down. He searches in the dead of winter for very practical reasons. "Winter is when evergreens stand out and can be easily noticed," he says.

Rockefeller Center's tree of choice is always a Norway spruce, a fast-growing tree that not only grows up—to as high as 130 feet—but also out, its side branches arcing gracefully. Size and shape make the Norway perfect for its role as the tree, the one all of America will see on their televisions throughout the holiday season.

The problem, says Murbach, is that the tree is quite rare in this part of the world. Norway spruces, as their name implies, are not native to North America. They come from the cool, fairly high regions of northern Europe and are not found in American forests at all. So when Murbach sets out to look for the year's Norway spruce, he looks in backyards and on front lawns, places where the trees might have been planted ornamentally and where sun and space have helped them grow tall and dense.

In making his search, mostly in the northeastern states, Murbach travels by car and by helicopter. The search is methodical, and these days, fairly high tech. Murbach carries a laptop equipped with a Global Positioning System, with which he can pinpoint the location of a likely-looking specimen. He jots down descriptions of any tree he locates, finding this one too short, another perhaps too narrow, but making a note to check back on them in a year or so.

By April, if nothing has turned up, the search becomes a bit frantic. Other trees are beginning to leaf out, and evergreens are obscured. Murbach intensifies his search, and by midsummer, aware that he is lucky to find even one appropriate specimen, he zeroes in on the homeowner whose tree is about to become famous.

Murbach "talks the family through it," in his words. There's no need, of course, to explain why he wants the tree; the tradition of the Rockefeller Center tree is known worldwide. But for any family, the process of giving the tree—with all the attendant publicity—is a big thing, and Murbach wants it to be a positive experience. So he urges the family to think carefully and deliberately.

No financial compensation is offered. "We try to keep all of it non-commercial," he says. Instead, he puts it to the family that their Norway spruce can be "a gift from them to New York City, really to the world."

**Rockefeller Center's tree of choice is always a Norway spruce, a fast-growing tree that not only grows up—to as high as 130 feet—but also out, its side branches arcing gracefully.**

To be sure, there are benefits beyond the giving. An overgrown Norway spruce in your front yard can be a lightning rod or a sun-blocking nuisance. Taking such a tree down can be a major and expensive undertaking. Rockefeller Center will do it for free and make sure the family's yard looks undisturbed afterward. For the most part, people are happy to do it, proud to be associated with the world-famous festivities surrounding the tree. In fact, says Murbach, "this is one of those all-nice stories."

Once the family has agreed, a special nursery team comes in to fertilize the tree, irrigate it, "clean it up," then truss it in preparation for its move. The team may have to shore up a driveway to ensure they can get the tree out. Or replant grass, or even move an outbuilding or shed. Whatever it takes, they do.

Finally, it is cut down, very carefully, and lowered onto a specially designed flatbed truck that extends like a telescope to accommodate its length. Because of the sheer size of the truck and its cargo—a very wide load—the tree is moved at night when traffic is minimal. "So far," says Murbach, "we've been lucky with bridges and such, although one narrow bridge nearly stopped us cold."

The truck pulls up on West 49th Street in Manhattan, on the south side of Rockefeller Center, where a telescoping crane lifts it into position just behind the gold statue of Prometheus, overlooking the ice-skating rink. Scaffolding is then erected all around the tree, and the electrical crew climbs up and clothes the tree with the 27,000 to 30,000 lights it wears, depending on its size. Unlike the typical home Christmas tree, entwined by ropes of lights, the lights for the Rockefeller Center tree are placed along each branch. Traditionally, there are five colors of lights. Only once was tradition broken: in December 2001 the colors red, white, and blue carried the memory of September 11 along with holiday greetings.

"The tree is a catalyst," says Murbach. "It brings people together. And it provides a sense of continuity."

**Scaffolding is erected all around the tree, and the electrical crew climbs up and clothes the tree with the 27,000 to 30,000 lights it wears, depending on its size.**

## Sardi's Caricatures, Strokes of Genius

**Sardi's caricatures,** those quirky line drawings that watch over Broadway diners, confer a kind of immortality on their subjects. Yes, it's great to win a Tony or an Oscar or a Pulitzer Prize. But seeing yourself on the wall of this landmark means you've really arrived; you've joined a unique pantheon of celebrities.

Richard Baratz is the fourth official caricaturist at Sardi's. He won the job in a contest run by the restaurant, then worried that he had lost it when the subject of his very first caricature hated his portrayal of her.

What Baratz didn't know was that the renowned entertainer was notorious for disliking almost all representations of herself. She would have hated her portrait if Renoir had painted it.

Baratz went on to his second assignment, Anthony Hopkins, who loved his caricature, and he's been on the job ever since.

And what a job it is. Baratz remembers with great fondness the gallantry and courtliness of Richard Burton, then starring on Broadway in *Equus,* while sitting for his sketch . . . the elegance and warmth of Myrna Loy . . . the charm of Jerry Stiller. He remembers what a thrill it was to meet Elizabeth Taylor . . . to spend time with composer Marvin Hamlisch . . . to exchange pleasantries with

George Hamilton when he starred on Broadway in *Chicago.* Hamilton, Baratz reports, is "very nice and very tan."

The people caricatured for Sardi's walls are predominantly, but not exclusively, show business performers. For reasons of proximity alone, Broadway theater stars rank first and foremost, but the giants of film, music, television, and dance are here as well. And not just performers. Managers, press agents and publicists, writers, directors, producers all find a place on the restaurant's walls.

Some non-showbiz types have also won a place. Helen Keller was one such. Cartoonist Al Capp was another.

Baratz's method for creating a caricature sounds simple enough. After restaurant management has conferred the honor and made the first call to the chosen celebrity, Baratz follows up with a phone call asking for an appointment. During the appointment, he takes photos—profile, three-quarter profile, full portrait—and talks with the person, trying to get an idea of the personality.

That insight, crucial to a successful caricature, is not always easy. For one thing, "I sometimes only get about 30 seconds of a person's time," Baratz says with slight exaggeration. That time is often in a dressing room just before a show, when the individual is concentrating on the performance to come, usually distracted. On the other hand, some subjects give him plenty of time. "I almost had dinner with Katharine Hepburn," he reports.

But some individuals are guarded, giving little, whether in 30 uncomfortable seconds or 30 leisurely minutes of posing for photographs. They seem uneasy with the idea of a caricature and uncooperative with the process.

Whatever he extracts from the interview, Baratz takes home with him to his studio, where he studies the photos, thinks, ponders, and begins to draw. He tries, he says, to "feel the spirit of the person" as he looks for that certain something—a look in the eye, the way a person laughs—that, in exaggeration, will suggest the spirit and reveal the personality.

Baratz creates three or four pencil sketches for a first pass by Sardi co-owner Max Klimavicius, who chooses the one he thinks should be completed for the wall.

It takes from three to five days to complete a caricature, Baratz says, although some come easier than others. He starts by penciling the sketch to size. Then he inks the sketch. And finally, he colors the caricature with an opaque paint known as gouache. The very last step is for the subject of the caricature to approve the work and autograph it.

Approval does not always come quickly or easily. Some celebrities, like the subject of Baratz's first caricature, can be difficult. He understands their hesitancy to see themselves caricatured. "These people make a living on their appearance," he says. It's less vanity than an instinct to protect the franchise, so to say, that makes them focus like

**He tries, he says, to "feel the spirit of the person" as he looks for that certain something—a look in the eye, the way a person laughs—that, in exaggeration, will suggest the spirit and reveal the personality.**

183

lasers on any representation, particularly one that sets out to exaggerate and distort for effect.

Whatever the problems, Baratz loves doing the Sardi's caricatures. "Drawing celebrities is fun," he says simply. He takes pleasure in the excitement that surrounds his subjects and is amused by the glory that sometimes attaches to him by reflection. There was the time a security guard parted the crowd to create a pathway as he entered the theater to sketch Burton, and the time he emerged from an interview with Cathy Huffman through *The Producers'* stage door and a whispered query hissed through the crowd: Who is that?

Why it's Richard Baratz. The famous caricaturist, of course.

## The Thanksgiving Day Parade: Kangaroos and Santa Claus

**The "longest-running show on Broadway,"** as it bills itself, is the Macy's Thanksgiving Day Parade. And with a 1924 starting date, it has a legitimate claim to that title.

There's no real equivalent anywhere to this parade. It combines music, art, acting, and performances, costumes, a telecast, celebrities,

and an audience of millions— an untold number of television viewers plus the people lining the parade route.

To bring off this extravaganza, it takes a staff of 40 people, working year-round. Half the staff—like producer/director Robin Hall and creative director Bill Schermerhorn, work out of the giant store's Manhattan location. The other half consists of artists, designers, carpenters, welders, electricians, and the people who create the giant balloons— balloonatics, they are called—who inhabit the Macy's studio in Hoboken, New Jersey, a two-story former Tootsie Roll factory. The studio is where the floats and balloons for the parade are designed, engineered, and built.

Thinking up parade ideas is an ongoing occupation. The parade has always had one overriding theme—"Entertainment for Children Everywhere." But around that general theme certain elements predominate each year. The seventy-fifth anniversary parade, for example, was dominated by nostalgia; in November 2001, the overriding element was patriotic.

As Schermerhorn says, "The parade is a living organism." It's a reflection of American popular culture, which is always yielding to new fashions and moods, so the staff constantly explores emerging trends: What the kids are looking at these days, what their parents are paying attention to.

Studio staff translate the new ideas into new floats—some four to eight per year—and into the helium balloons made of polyurethane-coated nylon that are the parade's signature. The balloons are big, too big even for the huge, loftlike space where they are filled with air for testing throughout the year, so the testing must proceed in stages, and the balloons are never fully inflated till parade time.

The production process makes it clear why almost all the executives of the production staff have theatrical backgrounds. Although it's not like a written play, the parade always tells a story. It starts with Thanksgiving and ends with Christmas. Along the way, there are emotional waves, moments when a pop singer is performing, times when a ballad is called for, others when a band blares. So Schermerhorn and his team must build an arc, just as a playwright or director would—from the opening-act turkey, through the song-and-dance routine on the showboat float, through the pauses for bumblebees and kangaroos gamboling along the parade route, through those peak points when the characters-of-the-moment balloons hover above the route, to the expected but always exciting grand finale when Santa's sleigh, accompanied by elves, makes its way down Broadway.

There was a time in the early days when the then much smaller balloons were released at the end of the parade and would float over the city for days. Eventually they'd come down, and some lucky child would have a new toy. Times have changed, but the Thanksgiving Day parade only gets more popular over the years.

**Studio staff translate the new ideas into new floats—some four to eight per year—and into the helium balloons made of polyurethane-coated nylon that are the parade's signature.**

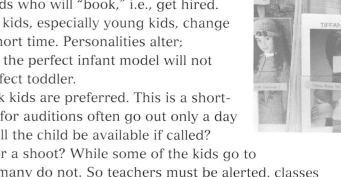

## Making It as a Child Model— It Helps to Live Here

**Photos are definitely the way to go to get attention. The staff does faithfully look at every picture that comes in. They are as anxious to find the right children as parents are to submit them.**

**Here's a secret,** but be careful how you spread it around. Your adorable little tot has a better chance of breaking into the big time as a child model if you live in the five boroughs than if you live in, say, Chicago or L.A.

It's not that New York has a premium on beautiful children. It's that Madison Avenue casts and shoots most of its ads here. Availability is crucial for any model, but even more so for the little ones, who must cope with school and child labor laws, in addition to bad hair days.

"We *love* kids from the city," says Marlene Wallach, who heads Wilhelmina Kids and Creative Management. Wilhelmina is, of course, one of the world's top modeling agencies. And its Kids' division is every bit as successful and influential as the mother branch.

Wallach and her staff of four spend a good part of their working days looking at photos of children that hopeful parents send in to them. Photos are definitely the way to go to get attention. The staff does faithfully look at every picture that comes in. They are as anxious to find the right children as parents are to submit them. There is a constant need for kids who will "book," i.e., get hired. As any parent knows, kids, especially young kids, change drastically in a very short time. Personalities alter; dimensions shift. And the perfect infant model will not necessarily be the perfect toddler.

And yes, New York kids are preferred. This is a short-notice business. Calls for auditions often go out only a day or two in advance. Will the child be available if called? Will he be available for a shoot? While some of the kids go to professional schools, many do not. So teachers must be alerted, classes made up.

Even for New York kids, the pickings are not easy. There are a lot of adorable kids clustered in the boroughs and thereabouts. And many, many of them have savvy parents who wouldn't mind a little help with the college tuition.

How are the lucky few chosen? What does it take to make it as a child model, beyond cute?

"It's personality," Wallach says emphatically. "Maybe it's a look in the eye; maybe it's an amazing smile. Something that's attractive to people, that engages them."

Because "personality" is such an ephemeral quality, Wilhelmina has an informal review committee that looks over the photos,

double-checking their impressions about any given child.

These days, there is more demand than ever for child models. Because of television, that small box that has had so much influence on our lives, children themselves become consumers at a much earlier age than a generation ago. Five-, four-, even three-year-olds can be very specific about what toy they want, and in what color. And let's not even get into the clothes market, where only the right brand of jeans or boots or hair decorations will be tolerated.

Beyond the ads directed to kids themselves are ads directed to adults but that feature kids. Advertisers have learned that our child-centered culture responds favorably to almost anything that hints it will make our kids happier, healthier, or safer.

Just as there are trends in the looks of adult models, there are trends in child models, too. Pretty is always in, says Wallach. You can't

**Pretty is always in, says Wallach. You can't go wrong with pretty. But these days pretty has a wider definition.**

go wrong with pretty. But these days pretty has a wider definition. It includes not only freckle-faced Caucasian kids but also non-Caucasians and, more recently, kids of "mixed ethnicity"—mixed race kids who a few years ago would not have been booked. So, to the extent that advertising reflects our culture, America seems to be becoming more broad-minded.

To fill all this demand, Wilhelmina keeps a steady stable of some 200 Wilhelmina Kids, with a core of 75 or so who get most of the work. Parents are very important in the lives of child models, she says. Usually, though not always, it's the parent who encourages the child to begin modeling and who holds his or her hand through all the ups and downs that follow.

And what of those ups and downs, especially the downs? The ad not booked, the polite rejection. Do they leave lasting scars? No one knows for sure, of course, but there is a self-selection process that operates early in the process. Kids who don't want to go on auditions, who would rather be playing football or dolls, or who don't like strangers looking them over, simply opt out. Remember trying to get your four-year-old to do something he didn't want to do?

The children that remain, Wallach says, seem not to be bothered by the vagaries of the business. "People are typically surprised," she says, by the atmosphere at auditions and "go sees," which are less formal than the audition. There's little evidence of the pushy stage mothers and manipulated children we've all seen in Hollywood movies. Few parents are so ill-mannered, and the kids actually seem to be relaxed, laid back, and having fun.

It's rare for child models to become grown-up models. The grown-up version has stringent height and weight and size requirements that narrow the field. Some kid models, of course, do grow up to go into show business. Jodie Foster is a prime example.

It is a lucrative way for a child to spend spare time, though not as lucrative as adult modeling. There are few "stars" among child models, few tiny Cindy Crawfords. Mostly there isn't enough time to build that kind of recognition. Occasionally a child will land a gig as the spokesperson for some product and do really well. Most kids earn somewhere between $75 to $125 per hour for fashion and beauty work, plus bonuses if the ad is used widely. Commercials can bring more. It's nice change for anyone.

And for the child who is so inclined, it is fun to dress up and pose for the camera, to be the center of so much attention. No wonder many kids, not just New York kids, want to try it.

To be certain everyone who deserves a chance gets one, Wilhelmina invites a carefully chosen few children from around the country to come to New York each summer. The children are chosen carefully to avoid having a child with marginal chances incur unnecessary expense. Wallach, who combines the professional's no-nonsense approach with a seemingly genuine concern for her little charges, is clear in spelling out the rules of the invitation. No expenses are paid, but the firm does agree to represent the child on an exclusive basis for that summer. Then the child is put up for bookings and everyone waits to see what happens.

Wallach remembers one little out-of-towner, a girl, who had winningly good looks and a personality that leaped out from her photo. But she also had a mouthful of shiny new braces. The braces, Wallach thought, would be a problem. Still . . . there was that knockout look.

She offered the summer contract to the girl and her mother, but—as she puts it—was "extremely discouraging. I said the braces would hold her back, that the summer would be expensive. I really laid it out."

In true showbiz fashion, Madison Avenue loved the little girl, braces and all. She booked like crazy, and suddenly had a promising career ahead of her.

Or, you might say, she came into town a nobody and left it a star.

It can happen only in New York.